CONTEMPORARY JAPANESE ARCHITECTS

CONTEMPORARY JAPANESE ARCHITECTS

BY DIRK MEYHÖFER

BENEDIKT TASCHEN

Frontispiece · Frontispiz · Frontispice
Kiko Mozuna: »Earth« Gallery

**This book was printed on 100% chlorine-free bleached
paper in accordance with the TCF standard.**

© 1994 Benedikt Taschen Verlag GmbH
Hohenzollernring 53, D-50672 Köln

By Dirk Meyhöfer, Hamburg
Design: QART (Brodda, Hierholzer, Klaus), Hamburg
Cover design: Angelika Muthesius, Cologne; Mark Thomson, London
Text edited by Barbro Garenfeld Büning, Cologne
English translation: Roger Rosko, Cologne
French translation: Frédérique Daber, Cahors

Printed in Italy
ISBN 3-8228-9442-7

CONTENTS

CURRENTS IN CONTEMPORARY JAPANESE ARCHITECTURE

AKTUELLE ARCHITEKTURSTRÖMUNGEN IN JAPAN

COURANTS ARCHITECTURAUX CONTEMPORAINS

by Katsuhiro **Kobayashi**

The contemporary architecture of Japan thrives on its incomparable diversity. It is conspicuous for its high quality, regardless of the conception or style represented. Together these two aspects have brought it to a standard within the world's architectural scene which is, without exaggeration, at the pinnacle. Japanese architecture received the thrust it needed to attain this level in the course of the last ten years.

Alongside the »first generation«, the great four – Arata Isozaki, Fumihiko Maki, Kazuo Shinohara and Kisho Kurokawa, born between 1925 and 1934, having completed their training shortly after the end of World War II and enjoying great success in their work for over thirty years – a second, younger generation has arisen. Until about 1980 the latter were in a kind of experimental phase, attempting to blaze new trails in residential design, or in search of a style of their own. The breakthrough onto the international stage came during the Eighties, after they had found their individual paths and smaller projects were followed by larger ones.

Tadao Ando, Toyo Ito, Itsuko Hasegawa, Kijo Rokkaku and Kiko Mozuna were all born in 1941; Katsuhiro Ishii, Riken Yamamoto and Shin Takamatsu a few years later. Over the last 15 years the two generations of architects have been working along-

Die zeitgenössische Architektur in Japan lebt von ihrer unvergleichlichen Vielfalt. Hinzu kommt ihre hohe Qualität, gleich welche Auffassung und welcher Stil vertreten werden. Beides zusammen hat zu einem Standard innerhalb der modernen Architektur geführt, der ohne Übertreibung an der Weltspitze rangiert. Den entscheidenden Schub zu dieser Entwicklung hat Japans Architektur in den letzten zehn Jahren erhalten.

Neben der »ersten Generation«, den großen Vier – Arata Isozaki, Fumihiko Maki, Kazuo Shinohara und Kisho Kurokawa, geboren zwischen 1925 und 1934 –, die kurz nach Kriegsende ihre Ausbildung abgeschlossen haben und seit über dreißig Jahren mit großem Erfolg bauen, ist eine zweite, jüngere Generation herangewachsen. Sie befand sich bis etwa 1980 in einer Art Experimentierphase, versuchte neue Wege im Wohnungsbau zu gehen oder war auf der Suche nach ihrem eigenen Stil. Der internationale Durchbruch kam in den achtziger Jahren, als sie ihren Weg gefunden hatte und den kleineren Projekten größere folgten.

Tadao Ando, Toyo Ito, Itsuko Hasegawa, Kijo Rokkaku und Kiko Mozuna sind alle 1941 geboren, Katsuhiro Ishii, Riken Yamamoto und Shin Takamatsu wenige Jahre später. In den letzten 15 Jahren haben also zwei Architektengenerationen gleichzeitig

L'architecture contemporaine japonaise vit d'un foisonnement formidable. A ceci s'ajoute, quel que soit le style ou le parti pris artistique, la qualité des créations. Quantité et qualité ont suscité un standard qui, soit dit sans exagération, est le premier au monde. C'est au cours des dix dernières années que l'architecture japonaise a connu un essor décisif.

A côté de la «première génération», celle des Quatre Grands: Arata Isozaki, Fumihiko Maki, Kazuo Shinohara et Kisho Kurokawa, qui sont nés entre 1925 et 1934, ont terminé leurs études peu après la guerre et qui construisent avec succès depuis plus de trente ans, une deuxième génération est apparue. Jusqu'en 1980, elle vécut sa phase d'expérimentation, tentant de renouveler la notion d'habitat ou cherchant son style. La reconnaissance internationale vint dans les années 80: chacun s'était trouvé, aux petits projets succédaient les grands. Tadao Ando, Toyo Ito, Itsuko Hasegawa, Kijo Rokkaku et Kiko Mozuna sont tous nés en 1941. Katsuhiro Ishii, Riken Yamamoto et Shin Takamatsu, quelques années plus tard. Durant ces quinze dernières années, deux générations d'architectes ont travaillé côte à côte, ce qui, évidemment, est une des raisons pour lesquelles l'architecture japonaise contemporaine a connu un essor si remarquable précisément pendant cette période. Ce

Tracking the Japanese past: View
of ceiling in Sukiya-yu Residence
(Katsuhiro Ishii, 1989)

Auf den Spuren der japanischen Vergangenheit: Decken-
untersicht in der Sukiya-yu-
Residenz (Katsuhiro Ishii, 1989)

Sur les traces du passé: vue plon-
geante du plafond de la Résidence
Sukiya-yu (Katsuhiro Ishii, 1989)

side each other. This fact is certainly one reason why the contemporary Japanese architecture has experienced a surge in quality during this period. Presented in this volume are the architects setting the standards for this epoch.

Coexistence

The following question remains to be answered: Why have the architectural developments in Japan yielded such varying results?

First of all, it is an outgrowth of the sociocultural conditions of the Japanese Empire, where traditional and modern models of existence abide alongside each other. Virtually everything connected with tradition in Japan enjoys extensive protection. In the process, members of the society want not only to conserve their traditions, they also wish to develop them further. Their mutually experienced history and handed-down ways of life form the basis of Japanese perception and sentiment. Thus, for example, the Japanese, and particularly the architects among them, have retained a high degree of sensitivity to traditional, primarily natural building materials like wood. Exactly the same is true of their love for simplicity of form, as has been evident for decades in their domestic arts and crafts, which have made their appearance as »Japanism« in Western cultural circles.

nebeneinander gearbeitet; darin liegt natürlich ein Grund, warum die zeitgenössische japanische Architektur gerade in dieser Zeit einen Qualitätssprung gemacht hat. In diesem Buch werden die maßgebenden Architekten dieser Epoche vorgestellt.

Koexistenz

Bleibt die Frage zu beantworten, warum die Architekturentwicklung in Japan recht unterschiedliche Ergebnisse mit sich gebracht hat.

Zuerst einmal liegt das an der soziokulturellen Situation des japanischen Kaiserreiches. Hier existieren traditionelle und moderne Leitbilder nebeneinander. In Japan steht alles das, was mit Tradition zu tun hat, unter weitgehendem Schutz. Dabei wollen alle Gesellschaftsmitglieder das Erbe nicht nur konservieren, sondern auch weiterentwickeln. Die gemeinsam erlebte Geschichte und die überkommenen Lebensformen bilden die Basis der japanischen Empfindungen und Regungen. So haben sich beispielsweise Japaner und vor allem die Architekten unter ihnen eine hohe Sensibilität für traditionelle, vor allem natürliche Baumaterialien wie Holz erhalten. Genauso erging es der Liebe zur einfachen Form, wie sie seit Jahrzehnten beim heimischen Kunsthandwerk zu beobachten ist, das als »Japonismus« Einzug in die westlichen Kulturkreise gehalten hat.

livre en présente les principaux artisans.

Coexistence

Pourquoi, tout au long de son évolution, l'architecture japonaise a-t-elle connu des résultats si différents?

Un des éléments de réponse est la situation socio-culturelle de l'empire japonais où coexistent des modèles traditionnels et modernes. Au Japon, tout ce qui se rapporte à la tradition fait l'objet de solides mesures de protection.

De plus, tous les citoyens aiment leur tradition au point de vouloir la conserver et même la prolonger. Cette histoire commune et les pratiques de vie héritées du passé forment la base de l'affectivité nationale. Ainsi les Japonais, et parmi eux surtout les architectes, sont-ils restés attachés aux matériaux de construction traditionnels, et avant tout à ceux qui sont naturels, comme par exemple le bois. Même chose pour l'amour de la forme simple que l'on observe depuis des décennies dans l'artisanat et qui a également conquis les faveurs de l'Occident.

Les Japonais ressentent le vide différemment des Occidentaux. Les notions d'«espace», de «périphérie» n'ont rien d'évident pour un Occidental tandis que «l'art du rien construit» fait partie intégrante de l'architecture japonaise moderne.

Even today the Japanese perceive an empty space differently than people of the Western hemisphere. »Gap« and »spell« devote an experience that the West is not easily able to grasp. The »art of constructed nothingness« is present, in latent form, throughout modern Japanese architecture.

On the other hand, Japan has hardly closed its eyes to the 20th century, with its electronic possibilities, the progress of the worldwide information society and its media, and other chal-

Japaner empfinden auch heute eine leere Fläche anders als die Menschen der westlichen Hemisphäre, »Zwischenraum« und »Bannkreis« umschreiben ein Erlebnis, das der Westen nicht ohne weiteres nachvollziehen kann. Die »Kunst des gebauten Nichts« ist latent in der modernen japanischen Architektur vorhanden.

Andererseits verschließt sich Japan nicht den Einflüssen des 20. Jahrhunderts, seiner elektronischen Möglichkeiten, des Fortschritts der weltweiten Informationsgesellschaft und ihrer

Par ailleurs, le Japon ne se ferme pas aux courants du 20ème siècle, à ses potentialités électroniques, aux progrès d'une société qui, grâce à ses médias, fait circuler l'information dans le monde entier, bref, à la modernité en ce qu'elle a d'agréable ou de moins agréable. Autant de forces qui s'exercent dans l'architecture japonaise, qui la font s'exprimer et lui donnent à réfléchir. Toyo Ito est probablement l'architecte qui a poussé le plus loin cet exercice, avec son Nomad Club, à Tokyo, qu'il a dédié à une société cos-

lenges of the present day – whether appealing or unwelcome. Each of these has influenced Japanese archi-tecture, compelling it to both reflection and expression. Toyo Ito is probably the one architect who has developed this process the furthest. A prime ex-ample of this is the Nomad Club in Tokyo, incorporating a light, tent-like temporary structure, which Ito dedi-cated to the roving cosmopolitan so-ciety.

This highly individualistic coexistence of traditional and modern influences is an important motor for the plurality found in Japan's contemporary archi-tecture. As long as this situation per-sists – presumably for a considerable period – its complexity and diversity will be retained, and perhaps even increase.

Medien und Herausforderungen von heute. All dies wirkt auf die japanische Architektur, zwingt sie zu Reflexionen und Äußerungen. Toyo Ito ist wahr-scheinlich der Architekt, der diese Vorgehensweise am weitesten voran-getrieben hat. Er tat dies beispiels-weise mit dem Nomad Club in Tokio, den er der vagabundierenden kos-mopolitischen Gesellschaft von heute gewidmet hat, und der die leichte und vorläufige Struktur eines Zeltes auf-nimmt.

Die eigenwillige Koexistenz von Tradi-tion und Moderne ist ein wichtiger Motor für die Pluralität in der heutigen Architektur Japans. Solange diese Si-tuation anhält – vermutlich wird sie es noch für eine geraume Zeit – werden sich Komplexität und Vielfalt erhalten, vielleicht noch steigern.

mopolite et vagabonde et dont la structure, légère, provisoire, est celle d'une tente.

La coexistence persistante de tradi-tion et de modernité est un moteur puissant de l'architecture japonaise. Tant que cette situation existera – et il est à prévoir que ce sera le cas encore longtemps – complexité et diversité perdureront ou peut-être même iront en augmentant.

Métropoles provisoires

Au Japon, l'architecture n'est pas seulement composite, elle est aussi sans cesse en mouvement, pour des raisons qui tiennent autant au passé qu'au présent. Par exemple, les tradi-tions ayant disparu du Japon urbain, les architectes ne se sentent pas bri-dés par les structures existantes. Pour-tant cette remarque n'est pas absolu-ment exacte: Tokyo, comme d'autres villes japonaises, possédait jusqu'à la Seconde Guerre mondiale, une sil-houette propre qui lui était caractéri-stique. Mais la reconstruction qui sui-vit ne rendit pas, comme en Europe ou sur la côte est des Etats-Unis, de con-texte historique. On a par conséquent l'impression que les villes japonaises ne sont que du provisoire. De nos jours, en Europe, on n'obtient pas de permis de construire pour des bâti-ments choquants ou mal intégrés. Dans une ville japonaise, le problème ne se pose même pas.

Temporary Metropolis

Japan's architecture is not only multi-layered, it is also in a state of constant flux. This can be explained in the light of both past and present. For one thing, Japan no longer has a metropolitan tradition, with the result that architects perceive no reason to take structures into consideration that have developed over the years. Of course, this assertion is not entirely accurate, since Tokyo and other Japanese cities had evolved an urban image up until the Second World War. No historical context of the sort found in Europe or on the East Coast of the United States can be discerned in Japan's post-war reconstruction. The impression one gathers that Japanese cities are merely provisional is quite justified. Today in Europe, no building would be permitted that infringed on the »genius loci« or failed to take it into account. This question seems to be of little importance in a Japanese city.

In fact, as a matter of general principle the Japanese do not construct their buildings and cities for eternity. Even their temples are not supposed to exist for more than a brief period, perhaps thirty years. Lurking behind this fact is a certain intention. The notion of »periodic reconstruction« is spoken of in Shinto architecture. The Ise Shrine, the most significant Shinto sanctuary, is replaced at regular intervals by a painstaking reconstruction, since in

Provisorische Großstadt

Japans Architektur ist nicht nur vielschichtig, sie ist auch immer in Bewegung. Das läßt sich sowohl aus der Vergangenheit als auch aus der Gegenwart erklären. Japan hat beispielsweise keine Großstadttradition mehr. Deswegen sehen die Architekten auch keinen Anlaß, auf gewachsene Strukturen Rücksicht zu nehmen. Ganz richtig ist diese Behauptung nicht, denn Tokio verfügte genauso wie andere japanische Städte bis zum Zweiten Weltkrieg über ein gewachsenes Stadtbild. Der Wiederaufbau nach dem Krieg läßt keinen geschichtlichen Kontext wie in Europa oder an der amerikanischen Ostküste erkennen. Japanische Städte, so der berechtigte Eindruck, sind nichts anderes als ein Provisorium. In Europa werden heute keine Gebäude zugelassen, die den »Genius loci« verletzen oder nicht berücksichtigen. Den japanischen Stadtplanern scheint das gleichgültig zu sein.

Japaner bauen grundsätzlich ihre Häuser und Städte nicht für die Ewigkeit. Selbst die Tempelbauten sollen in Japan immer nur für eine kurze Dauer, vielleicht für dreißig Jahre, bestehen. Dahinter verbirgt sich eine Philosophie: In der Shinto-Architektur spricht man vom »periodischen Neubau«. Der Ise-Schrein, das bedeutendste Shinto-Heiligtum, wird regelmäßig durch eine exakte Rekonstruktion er-

C'est par principe que les Japonais ne construisent pas leur maison pour l'éternité. Même les temples ne sont conçus que pour une courte durée, une trentaine d'années environ. L'architecture shinto parle en effet de «reconstruction périodique». Le sanctuaire d'Ise, le plus important des lieux de culte du shintoïsme, est régulièrement remplacé par sa propre réplique.

En effet, dans le shintoïsme ce n'est pas le durable qui est vénéré mais la beauté symbolique de la constante rénovation. De là cette souplesse des Japonais dans leur conception de la construction. Cette mentalité, alliée à la disparition de la ville japonaise pendant la guerre, a fait de ce pays un champ d'expérimentation extraordinaire pour l'architecture.

Pays du boom

Une autre raison de cette spécificité japonaise de l'architecture est la con-

Shintoism it is not the enduring that is revered – this would be contradictory to the religion's tenets – but rather the symbolic beauty of constant renewal. In this way a somewhat relaxed, peculiarly Japanese attitude has arisen regarding their edifices. A conception of this nature, combined with the disappearance of the earlier Japanese city during the war, has ultimately made Japan into a unique field for architectural experimentation.

Boom Country

One more reason for the particularity of Japanese architecture can be found in the economic boom the country has enjoyed in recent years, an unhealthily high flight accompanied by a financial glut and an insane inflation of land prices. In 1992

setzt, denn im Shintoismus wird nicht das Dauerhafte verehrt, weil das der Religion widersprechen würde, sondern das symbolisch Schöne der ständigen Erneuerung. Auf diese Weise entstand eine spezifisch lässige Haltung Bauwerken gegenüber. Eine derartige Auffassung zusammen mit der im Krieg verschwundenen japanischen Stadt hat Japan schließlich zu einem einzigartigen Experimentierfeld für Architektur werden lassen.

Boom Country

Ein weiterer Grund für die spezielle japanische Architektur ist in der Hochkonjunktur der letzten Jahre zu finden, eine ungesunde Hochkonjunktur, die von Geldüberfluß und einer immensen Inflation der Bodenpreise begleitet wurde. 1992 platzte die »Seifenblase«, die überhitzte Konjunktur erlitt einen existentiellen Rückschlag, und die Flaute wird einige Jahre andauern. Die Hochkonjunktur war dennoch für den Bauboom verantwortlich und weckte großes Interesse an der Architektur. Sie verhalf den Avantgardearchitekten (vor allem jenen, die in diesem Buch vorgestellt werden) zu größeren Aufträgen, und das galt für Büro- und Geschäftshäuser wie für öffentliche Bauten.

Die Hochkonjunktur erzielte noch einen Nebeneffekt. Nicht nur Japaner, sondern viele Architekten aus Übersee erhielten die Chance, in Japan zu

joncture économique des dernières années: une conjoncture pléthorique accompagnée d'une inflation incroyable du prix du terrain constructible.

Cette «bulle de savon» éclata en 1992. L'économie, chauffée à blanc, subit un recul et le ralentissement durera plusieurs années. Pourtant, ce sont ces conditions économiques favorables qui expliquent le boom de la construction et l'éveil d'un intérêt porté à l'architecture. Ce sont elles aussi qui procurèrent aux constructeurs d'avant-garde – présentés dans ce livre – des commandes importantes, aussi bien pour des immeubles de bureaux ou commerciaux que pour des édifices publics.

Effet secondaire de la conjoncture économique: ces dernières années, de nombreux architectes non-japonais eurent l'occasion de construire au Japon, ce qui, dix ans auparavant, eût paru invraisemblable. C'est ainsi que, lauréats de concours internationaux, l'Italien Renzo Piano signe le Kansai International Airport et Rafael Vignoli, le Tokyo Forum. Sous l'égide d'Arata Isozaki, huit constructeurs de renom (Rem Koolhaas, Christian de Portzamparc, Oscar Tusquets, entre autres) conçoivent «Nexusworld», à Fukuoka, bâtiments d'habitation à l'occidentale destinés aux Japonais. A l'heure actuelle, à la faveur de cette cassure provoquée par la crise, le

the »soap-bubble« popped. The overheated economy has suffered a drastic setback, and the current slack period will continue for several years. The economic boom was, nevertheless, responsible for a huge surge in construction, sparking a great deal of interest in architecture. It helped avant-garde architects to win larger commissions (particularly those portrayed in this book). This applies not only to office and commercial construction, but to public buildings as well.

The economic boom had one more side-effect. In recent years not only Japanese but also many architects from overseas have had an opportunity to execute their designs in Japan — something that would not have been imaginable only ten years ago. Thus, after winning international competitions, the Italian Renzo Piano designed the Kansai International Airport, and Rafael Vignoli the Tokyo Forum. Under the auspices of Isozaki, eight internationally acknowledged architects (including Rem Koolhaas, Christian de Portzamparc and Oscar Tusquets) designed »Nexusworld« in Fukuoka — Western residential construction for Japan.

Now, after the onset of an economic slump, there is a caesura — the right time to appraise a very important phase of recent Japanese architectural history.

bauen. Dies wäre vor etwa 10 Jahren undenkbar gewesen. So bauen der Italiener Renzo Piano den Kansai International Airport und Rafael Vignoli das Tokio Forum, weil sie internationale Wettbewerbe gewonnen haben. Unter der Ägide von Arata Isozaki haben acht renommierte Architekten (u. a. Rem Koolhaas, Christian de Portzamparc, Oscar Tusquets) Nexusworld in Fukuoka entworfen — westlicher Wohnungsbau für Japan. Jetzt, nach dem Konjunktureinbruch, entsteht eine Zäsur — der richtige Zeitpunkt zur Würdigung eines sehr wichtigen Abschnitts der neueren Architekturgeschichte.

moment est venu de rendre hommage à une période primordiale de l'histoire de l'architecture.

Géometrie et raffinement

Au cours de cette période on observe dans le domaine de la construction quatre principes de base qui marquent de leur empreinte la pensée et le style des architectes.

Le premier est la géométrie. Certes, en Occident aussi, on travaille à partir de formes géométriques mais dans les maisons et les temples japonais, motifs ou modules géométriques font partie du vocabulaire élémentaire. Tadao Ando utilise la géométrie de la

A new expressionism: Details of Origin I-III,
Kyoto (Shin Takamatsu, 1981–1986)

Ein neuer Expressionismus: Details aus
Origin I–III, Kioto (Shin Takamatsu, 1981–86)

Un nouvel expressionnisme: détail d'Origin
I-III, Kyoto (Shin Takamatsu, 1981–1986)

Geometry and Refinement

In the architecture of this period, four design principles can be discerned and named which are applied by Japanese architects and influence both construction methods and modes of thought.

Geometry is the most significant of them. The use of basic geometric forms as design parameters is, of course, also familiar in the West. However, geometric patterns or modules are a part of the ancient Japanese architectural vocabulary for both residence and temple.

Tadao Ando's use of geometric forms in design is rather conspicuous. His basic design grid is drawn from the »tatami«, the traditional rice-straw mat. He manipulates concrete blocks measuring 90 by 180 cm, meticulously lining them up next to each other – an homage to geometry and the grid.

Arata Isozaki also places his stakes on geometry: the square and the circle. He has committed himself to these forms since the Seventies (e. g. the museum in Gunma). Even during the phase in which he emulated historical models, becoming a trailblazer for post-modern architecture in Japan, he still had not lost sight of geometry as the measure of all things. Vigorous geometric forms are once again apparent in his most recent projects, including the Disney Building and the freshly-won competition for

Geometrie und Verfeinerung

Innerhalb der Architektur aus diesem Zeitabschnitt sind vier Entwurfsprinzipien zu erkennen und zu benennen, die von japanischen Architekten angewendet werden und die Bau- und Denkweise prägen.

Hauptprinzip ist die Geometrie. Geometrische Grundformen als Entwurfsparameter kennt man zwar auch im Westen, geometrische Muster oder Module gehören jedoch zum japanischen Urvokabular an Haus und Tempel. Einer, der sehr auffällig geometrische Formen verwendet, ist Tadao Ando. Sein Entwurfs-Grundraster ist dem Maß der »tatami«, der traditionellen Reisstrohmatte, entlehnt; er hantiert mit 90 mal 180 cm großen Betonteilen, die, akkurat nebeneinander gereiht, eine Hommage an Raster und Geometrie sind.

Auch Arata Isozaki setzt auf Geometrie, auf Quadrat und Kreis. Seit den

façon la plus flagrante. Sa grille, élément conceptuel, emprunte ses dimensions au «tatami», le tapis traditionnel en paille de riz. Il dispose ses morceaux de béton de 90 x 180 cm les uns à côté des autres en un hommage à la géométrie.

Arata Isozaki s'appuie lui aussi sur la géométrie et, depuis les années soixante-dix, il travaille à partir du carré et du cercle (comme c'est le cas pour le musée de Gunma, par exemple). Même pendant sa période postmoderne, pendant laquelle son inspiration lui venait du passé, il ne perd pas de vue la géométrie. Et dans ses projets les plus récents, comme son Disney Building en Floride ou les salles de concerts de Kyoto et de Nara, pour lesquels il fut choisi sur concours, on retrouve des formes géométriques. La conception de la géométrie de Arata Isozaki s'applique autant aux formes de base

concert halls in Kyoto and Nara. Isozaki's geometric conceptions are not limited to the basic forms alone: segments of them also come into play. His current buildings incorporate curved surfaces, thus becoming allusions to erotic motifs.

Kazuo Shinohara reveres geometry as well, even when he reserves the right to destroy the forms or sets them to battle against one another (see essay by Dirk Meyhöfer p. 39) in order to generate an ambivalence he considers fitting for this era.

Another central principle is refinement. Refining form and material is among the Japanese' most prominent aptitudes. The given vocabulary of

siebziger Jahren ist Isozaki diesen Formen verpflichtet (z. B. Museum in Gunma). Und selbst in jener späteren Werkphase, als er historischen Vorbildern nacheiferte und Vorreiter der postmodernen Architektur in Japan wurde, hat er die Geometrie als Maß aller Dinge nicht aus den Augen gelassen. In den jüngsten Projekten, dem Disney Building in Florida und den gerade gewonnenen Wettbewerben für Konzerthallen in Kioto und Nara, werden wieder geometrische Formen sichtbar. Isozakis Liebe zur Geometrie beschränkt sich nicht auf die Grundformen, sondern er verwendet auch geometrische Segmente. Seine Bauten setzen sich aus gekrümmten Flächen zusammen — und spielen so auf erotische Motive an.

Auch Kazuo Shinohara verehrt die Geometrie, selbst wenn er sich vorbehält, die Formen zu zerstören und gegeneinander kämpfen zu lassen (vgl. Essay von Dirk Meyhöfer, S. 39), um eine Ambivalenz zu erzeugen, die er für zeitgerecht hält.

Ein anderes Prinzip ist die Verfeinerung. Materialveredlung und Formverfeinerung sind die hervorragenden Begabungen der Japaner. Das vorgegebene Vokabular der modernen Architektur wird aufgenommen und weiterentwickelt. Fumihiko Maki heißt der Meister dieses Faches. Seine Bearbeitung des »Industrial vocabulary«, wie er es nennt, führt zu elegan-

qu'aux formes fragmentaires. Actuellement, ses constructions sont formées de surfaces courbes, à connotation érotique.

Kazuo Shinohara est, lui aussi, un adepte de la géométrie, même lorsqu'il s'applique à désintégrer les formes pour les affronter les unes aux autres (voir l'article de Dirk Meyhöfer, p. 40) avec l'idée de traduire une ambiguïté qui lui semble typique de l'époque.

Le second principe est le raffinement stylistique. L'emploi de matériaux précieux et le travail minutieux de la forme sont deux choses dans lesquelles les Japonais excellent. L'exercice consiste à employer le langage architectural moderne et de le pousser plus loin. Fumihiko Maki est passé maître dans cet art. Son interprétation de ce qu'il appelle «industrial vocabulary» donne des maisons élégantes qui se fondent dans le contexte de la métropole japonaise. Des exemples types en sont le Spiral Building à Tokyo et le Musée d'art de Kyoto.

Kisho Kurokawa travaille la notion d'espace, typiquement japonaise, en combinaison avec des détails d'origine occidentale et ses créations sont faites de ces deux tendances conjointes. Les proportions plus réduites de ses construction permettent des juxtapositions qui ne seraient pas possibles ailleurs.

Même Shin Takamatsu, un des archi-

Power lies in detail. Left page: Tokyo Budokan (Kijo Rokkaku, 1990); below: Syntax Building, Kyoto (Shin Takamatsu, 1990)

Die Stärke liegt im Detail. Linke Seite: Tokio Budokan (Kijo Rokkaku, 1990); unten: Syntax Building, Kioto (Shin Takamatsu, 1990)

C'est le détail qui compte: p. de gauche: Tokyo Budokan (Kijo Rokkaku, 1990); en bas: Syntax Building, Kyoto (Shin Takamatsu, 1990)

modern architecture is taken up and developed further. Fumihiko Maki is the master of this art. His cultivation of the industrial »vocabulary«, as he calls it, results in elegant buildings that are well adapted to the context of the Japanese metropolis. Some prime examples of these are his Spiral Building in Tokyo and the art museum in Kyoto. Kisho Kurokawa has been refining the Japanese conception of space while simultaneously taking a Western approach to detail, bringing them together in a single building. The application of more graceful criteria permits the coexistence of things that actually do not belong together.

Even Shin Takamatsu, one of the wildest of Japan's architects, has recently been adopting a more refined tone. The motifs he uses are primarily ones he developed on his own. The larger his projects are, the more refined his façades become.

Symbolism and Expressionism

Architecture as the symbol of a viewpoint or realization – this approach is probably the most important in Japan's current architectural scene.

Hiroshi Hara, for instance, attempts through his architecture to translate complex structures of human consciousness and, above all, natural phenomena like the aurora borealis or a dew drop. He calls this approach the »architecture of modality«. It is in-

ten Häusern, die sich dem Kontext der japanischen Großstadt anpassen. Beispiele sind das Spiral Building in Tokio und das Museum in Kioto.

Kisho Kurokawa verfeinert den japanischen Raumbegriff, verwendet aber gleichzeitig auch Details aus dem Westen und läßt sie an einem Gebäude zusammenleben. Der grazilere Maßstab ermöglicht dabei die Koexistenz von Dingen, die eigentlich nicht zusammengehören.

Selbst Shin Takamatsu, einer der wildesten Architekten Japans, schlägt inzwischen feinere Töne an, hauptsäch-

tectes les plus rebelles du Japon, donne à présent dans le raffinement, avec des motifs qu'il a, la plupart du temps, inventés lui-même. Plus ses projets deviennent importants, plus raffinées ses façades.

Symbolisme et expressionnisme

L'architecture comme manifestation d'une attitude ou d'une notion: voilà la tendance majeure de l'architecture japonaise.

Hiroshi Hara, par exemple, a l'ambition de traduire dans ses réalisations la complexité des processus de la

Homage to a mobile society: Nomad Club,
Tokyo (Toyo Ito, 1986)

Hommage an eine mobile Gesellschaft:
Nomad Club, Tokio (Toyo Ito, 1986)

Hommage à une société en mouvement:
Nomad Club, Tokyo (Toyo Ito, 1986)

tended to assure that people feel at home in his buildings, that architecture, nature and human consciousness are in harmony. Particularly his more recent large-scale projects, including the skyscraper in Umeda and the railway station in Kyoto, are designed according to this principle.

Toyo Ito uses other central conceptions, such as »simulated city« and »architecture reflective of wind«, though in practice he integrates nature into his buildings. In the Tower of Winds a computer program transforms the wind's direction and force into optical signals. Like the wind, his architecture is intended to be fresh and clear. Ito wants to build anything other than monuments, preferring to design »clothing« for people, which ought to become their soft, organic second skin. To stay with the metaphor, Ito treats architecture very much like fashion, always seeking something new and varying the style as he goes. Thus, changeability and transitoriness should be retained in the process. Therefore, Toyo Ito is, in the traditional sense, a very Japanese architect, due to the fact that traditional Japanese architecture draws its power and beauty from transformation and the new – not from permanence. Itsuko Hasegawa has also made nature her theme. In contrast to the buildings of Hiroshi Hara and Toyo Ito, all of which are kept very transpa-

lich mit Motiven, die er selbst entwikkelt hat. Je größer seine Projekte, desto feiner werden seine Fassaden.

Symbolik und Expressionismus

Architektur als Symbol für eine Haltung oder Erkenntnis – dieser Ansatz ist wohl der wichtigste in der derzeitigen Architekturszene Japans.
Hiroshi Hara beispielsweise will mit seiner Architektur komplizierte Bewußtseinsstrukturen der Menschen und vor allem Naturphänomene wie Polarlicht oder Tautropfen umsetzen. Er nennt das die »Architektur der Modalität«. Sie soll dafür sorgen, daß sich Menschen in seinen Häusern wohl fühlen und sich Architektur, Natur und menschliches Bewußtsein im Einklang befinden. Insbesondere seine neueren Großprojekte wie der Wolkenkratzer in Umeda und der Bahnhof von Kioto werden nach diesem Entwurfsprinzip gestaltet.
Toyo Ito verwendet andere Schlüsselbegriffe, wie »Simulated City« oder »Architecture reflective of wind«, aber er bindet auch die Natur in seine Häuser ein: Im Turm der Winde setzt ein Computerprogramm Windrichtung und -stärke in optische Signale um. Wie der Wind soll seine Architektur frisch und klar sein. Ito will alles andere, als Monumente bauen, eher »Kleider« für Menschen entwerfen, die sanft und organisch zur zweiten Haut werden sollen. Um im Bild zu

conscience humaine et, plus encore, des phénomènes naturels tels que la lumière polaire ou la rosée. Il appelle cela «l'architecture de la modalité». Elle doit permettre que l'homme se sente bien dans sa maison et qu'architecture, nature et concience humaine se rencontrent dans l'harmonie. Les plus récents travaux de l'architecte Hiroshi Hara, le gratte-ciel de Umeda ou la gare de Kyoto, par exemple, sont conçus à partir de ce principe.
Toyo Ito propose d'autres concepts, «simulated city», par exemple, ou «architecture reflective of wind» mais il fait intervenir la nature dans ses constructions. A la Tour des Vents, un programme informatique transforme direction et force du vent en signaux optiques. Comme le vent, son style architectural se veut frais et clair. Ito veut tout sauf créer des monuments. Il

Staged like a Disney production: Shonandai Cultural Center, Fujisawa (Itsuko Hasegawa, 1990). Right page top: Mobile leightweight house: Rotunda Building, Yokohama (Riken Yamamoto, 1987)

Inszenierung wie bei Disney: Shonandai-Kulturzentrum, Fujisawa (Itsuko Hasegawa, 1990). Rechte Seite oben: Mobiler Leichtbau: Haus Rotunda, Yokohama (Riken Yamamoto, 1987)

Mise en scène à la Disney: Centre culturel Shonandai, Fujisawa (Itsuko Hasegawa, 1990). Page de droite, en haut: Mobiles bâtiments: La Maison Rotunda, Yokohama (Riken Yamamoto, 1987)

rent and light, Hasegawa's projects evoke the impression of artificial nature. Her vigorous and fantasy-laden »natural worlds« create an atmosphere reminiscent of the American Disneyland.

Riken Yamamoto creates residential structures that harmonize with the lifestyle and joie-de-vivre of their inhabitants: appealing, transparent, mobile, lightweight buildings (the Rotunda Building in Yokohama, for instance) with opulent top storeys.

The expression of architects' individual sensibilities through form and figure in their respective work has already appeared in Expressionism, for example, as the temperament of the period was symbolized by the bizarre deformation of façades. A similar current has developed in present-day

bleiben: Ito behandelt Architektur durchaus wie Mode, er sucht immer nach etwas Neuem und ändert dabei den Stil. Wandelbarkeit und Vergänglichkeit sollen jedoch erhalten bleiben. Und weil die traditionelle japanische Architektur ihre Kraft und Schönheit auch aus dem Neuen bezieht und nicht etwa aus der Beständigkeit, ist Toyo Ito – im traditionellen Sinne – ein sehr japanischer Architekt.

Auch Itsuko Hasegawa hat die Natur zu ihrem Thema gemacht. Im Gegensatz zu Bauten von Hiroshi Hara und Toyo Ito, die alle sehr transparent und leicht gehalten sind, erwecken Hasegawas Projekte den Eindruck einer künstlichen Natur. Ihre kräftigen und phantasievollen »Naturwelten« erzeugen eine Atmosphäre, die an das amerikanische Disneyland erinnert.

voit ses créations comme des vêtements pensés pour des être humains, des secondes peaux, douces, organiques. Pour poursuivre la comparaison: l'architecture est pour Toyo Ito comme la mode, il cherche toujours la nouveauté, le changement de style. Tout doit pouvoir se transformer, disparaître au profit d'autre chose. Et comme l'architecture japonaise traditionnelle tient sa force et sa beauté de la nouveauté, non de la durabilité, Toyo Ito est, au sens traditionnel, un architecte extrêmement japonais.

Itsuko Hasegawa est elle aussi inspirée par la nature. Contrairement aux constructions de Hiroshi Hara et Toyo Ito, qui, toutes, gardent transparence et légèreté, les projets de Hasegawa évoquent une nature artificielle. Ses «mondes naturels», foisonnant de force et d'imagination, font penser au Disneyland américain.

Riken Yamamoto construit des maisons particulières faites pour refléter le style de vie de leurs habitants. Ce sont de joyeux petits bâtiments, transparents et mobiles (la Maison Rotunda, à Yokohama, en est un exemple), pourvus de terrasses très aménagées.

L'expressionnisme, déjà, avait commencé à vouloir exprimer des émotions au moyen de formes et de figures et ses façades tarabiscotées témoignent de l'ambiance de l'époque. Dans le Japon d'aujourd'hui, il existe

Japan, even though the thought involved is more formalist now. Shin Takamatsu confronts us with the martial façades of blades and halberds; Kiko Mozuna is also a leading exponent of the school. Certainly the latter's more recent buildings (e. g. Monzen Family Inn) no longer have quite the lurid, demonic aura of his earlier work, but nonetheless their figurative messages are still obvious; for instance, he uses the »figure« of an old Japanese building for the construction of guest-apartments.

Kijo Rokkaku aspires to a monumental form which is frequently arrived at through the complex assembly of simple forms, thus achieving an effect which ought not be called decorative, but rather dynamic. Atsushi Kitagawara, on the other hand, utilizes a vocabulary that is connected with the

Riken Yamamoto baut Wohnhäuser, die im Einklang mit dem Lebensstil und der Lebensfreude ihrer Bewohner sein sollen, freundliche, durchsichtige, mobile Leichtbauten (wie das Rotunda-Haus in Yokohama) mit opulenten Dachgeschossen.

Mit Formen und Figuren individuelle Empfindungen der Architekten in ihrer jeweiligen Architektur auszudrücken, diesen Ansatz hat es beispielsweise auch schon im Expressionismus gegeben, als die bizarre Verformung von Fassaden Gemütszustände der damaligen Zeit symbolisierten.

Im heutigen Japan hat sich eine ähnliche Strömung entwickelt, auch wenn jetzt formalistischer gedacht wird. Shin Takamatsu formuliert aus Schneiden und Hellebarden wehrhafte Fassaden, auch Kiko Mozuna ist ein führender Vertreter dieser Richtung. Zwar haben seine neueren Arbeiten (z. B. Monzen Family Inn) nicht mehr die düstere, dämonische Ausstrahlung seiner früheren Bauwerke, dennoch bleiben die figürlichen Botschaften ablesbar: Mozuna benutzt die »Figur« des alten japanischen Hauses für den Bau von Gästeapartments.

Kijo Rokkaku bevorzugt eine monumentale Form, die er häufig durch den komplizierten Zusammenbau einfacher Formen erzielt und damit einen eher dynamischen als dekorativen Effekt erreicht. Atsushi Kitagawara verwendet »Vokabeln« aus dem »Welt-

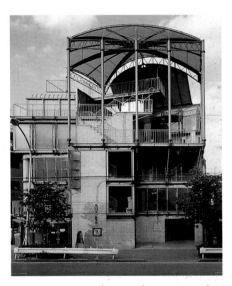

un courant analogue, bien que plus formellement structuré. Shin Takamatsu crée des façades défensives, hérissées de lames et de hallebardes et Kiko Mozuna est, lui aussi, un brillant représentant de cette école. Ses derniers travaux, la Monzen Family Inn, par exemple, n'ont plus l'esprit sombre et démoniaque de ses réalisations plus anciennes mais lorsqu'il utilise symboliquement la maison traditionnelle japonaise pour abriter les clients de l'hôtel, il l'investit d'un message formel.

Kijo Rokkaku recherche une forme monumentale qu'il obtient par la combinaison de formes simples pour un effet plus dynamique que décoratif. Atsushi Kitagawara, lui, parle une sortie du «scenario de fin du monde» des déconstructivistes. Pourtant, le dynamisme «hors-gravité» qui carac-

deconstructivists' »end of the world scenario«. However, Kitagawara avoids the anti-gravitational dynamism that characterizes of Western deconstructivism. He prefers a nihilistic mode of expression, placing his images in a thoroughly theatrical light (as with the Rise Building in Tokyo).

Outlook
Present-day architecture in Japan, represented in this book by thirteen architects, can be divided into these four currents: geometry, refinement, symbolism and expressionism. However, this is only one option among many; other classifications could be devised. The results will consistently reveal that the Japanese architectural scene is thoroughly heterogenous. Furthermore, it is quite fitting for Japan that several of its architects are staying in the course they have embarked on, while others are already visibly inclined to undertake new experiments. At present the so-called second postwar generation is in full bloom; the next, the third or baby-boomer generation of the Fifties, is on the starting line. Despite the present economic slump, there is much innovation to look forward to at the turn of the millenia.

untergangsszenario« der Dekonstruktivisten. Doch wird der anti-gravitierende Dynamismus, der den westlichen Dekonstruktivismus prägt, bei Kitagawara getilgt. Er bevorzugt eine nihilistische Ausdrucksweise, die seine Bilder ins rechte theatralische Licht rücken (Rise Building in Tokio).

Ausblick
Die aktuelle japa ische Architektur, hier vertreten durc 13 Architekten, in die vier Tendenzen Geometrie, Verfeinerung, Symbolik und Expressionismus aufzuteilen und dadurch ihre Stilauffassungen transparenter zu machen, ist eine Möglichkeit unter vielen. Man kann auch anders vorgehen. Die Erkenntnis wird immer sein, daß die japanische Architekturszene sehr heterogen ist. Und es paßt zu Japan, daß einige der Architekten ihre eingeschlagene Richtung einhalten werden, doch andere, schon jetzt sichtbar, zu neuen Experimenten neigen. Zur Zeit steht die zweite Nachkriegsgeneration in voller Blüte, die nächste, die dritte Generation der »Babyboomer« aus den fünfziger Jahren befindet sich an der Startlinie. Trotz des derzeitigen Konjunktureinbruchs ist zum Jahrtausendwechsel noch viel Neues zu erwarten.

térise ce mouvement est absent de l'œuvre de Kitagawara. Il lui préfère un style nihiliste que ses créations mettent en lumière d'une façon tout à fait théâtrale (Rise Building, à Tokyo).

Perspectives
Diviser l'architecture japonaise contemporaine, représentée ici par treize créateurs, en quatre tendances: géométrie, raffinement, symbolisme et expressionnisme pour tenter d'en expliquer les conceptions stylistiques, n'est qu'un choix parmi d'autres. Mais, quelle que soit la classification, il nous faut constater ce fait: le monde de l'architecture, au Japon, est très hétérogène: certains continuent sur leur lancée tandis que d'autres semblent prêts à de nouvelles expérimentations. Actuellement, la seconde génération de l'après-guerre est en pleine productivité tandis que la suivante, la troisième génération du baby boom, née dans les années cinquante, est à la ligne de départ. Malgré la mauvaise conjoncture économique, il y a beaucoup à attendre de ce changement de siècle.

Theatrical nihilism: Rise Building,
Tokyo (Atsushi Kitagawara, 1986)

Theatralischer Nihilismus: Rise Building,
Tokio (Atsushi Kitagawara, 1986)

Nihilisme théâtral: Rise Building, Tokyo
(Atsushi Kitagawara, 1986)

Coexistence of differing in-
fluences, from both East and West:
Hiroshima Museum of Art
(Kisho Kurokawa, 1988)

Zusammenleben unterschied-
licher Einflüsse – aus West und
Ost: Kunstmuseum Hiroshima
(Kisho Kurokawa, 1988)

Coexistence de courants divers venus de l'Ouest et de l'Est: musée
d'Hiroshima (Kisho Kurokawa,
1988)

THE JAPANESE MIRACLE – FROM A WESTERN VIEWPOINT

DAS JAPANISCHE WUNDER – AUS WESTLICHER SICHT

LE MIRACLE JAPONAIS – VU DE L'OCCIDENT

by Dirk **Meyhöfer**

The East glows, and Far Eastern avant-garde architecture's illustrious imago sets the West trembling: »Anything goes«. Bizarre backdrops like those of the best science-fiction films, archaic cult buildings, inconceivable high tech, and to top it off a mixture of them all together in one structure. Anything, so it seems from a distance, is thinkable, feasible, and can even be constructed—an »architectura nova«? The global style for the fin de siècle and following millenia?

Again and again Western visitors to Japan are brought to the extreme of their ability to absorb new impressions. Partially responsible for this is a pronounced delight in contradiction. The basic philosophy of the Japanese is »this as well as that«. The tea ceremony and the unbridled amusement district in Toyko; the ascetic posture of Buddhism or Shintoism and the hedonistic industrial society at the same time. And alongside an utterly unrestrained architecture of the future (at least in the rural areas) is the original Japanese building—an ascetic archetype abstaining from any ornamentation whatsoever.

Roots

Japanese tradition, in other words the society's roots, is a key piece of the Japanese puzzle. It is thus worthwhile to take a glance at and into the original Japanese house: a structure of un-

Der Osten leuchtet, und das illustre Imago fernöstlicher Architekturavantgarde läßt den Westen erschauern: »Anything goes«. Bizarre Kulissen wie aus besten Science-fiction-Filmen, archaische Kultbauten, unvorstellbares High Tech und als Krönung eine Mischung aus allem zusammen an einem Bauwerk. Alles, so scheint es aus der Ferne, ist denkbar, machbar und eben baubar – eine »architectura nova«? Der Weltstil für das Fin de siècle und das Jahrtausend danach? Westliche Besucher werden in Japan immer wieder an den Rand ihrer Aufnahmefähigkeit gebracht. Dafür mitverantwortlich ist die ausgeprägte Liebe zum Widerspruch. Die Grundphilosophie der Japaner heißt »sowohl als auch«: Teezeremonie und zügellose Amüsierviertel in Tokio; asketische Haltung des Buddhismus oder Shintoismus und hedonistische Industriegesellschaft zugleich. Und neben der haltlosen Zukunftsarchitektur, zumindest in den ländlichen Gebieten, das alte japanische Haus – ein asketischer Archetyp, der auf jegliches Ornament verzichtet.

Wurzeln

Die japanische Tradition, also die Wurzeln der Gesellschaft, bildet ein Schlüsselstück im japanischen Puzzle. Es lohnt sich, deswegen einen Blick auf und in das alte japanische Haus zu werfen: ein roh belassenes Holz-

L'Orient s'illumine et l'image de l'avant-garde architecturale de ces contrées lointaines fait frissonner l'Occident: «Anything goes». Décors étranges faits, semble-t-il, pour des films de science-fiction, lieux de culte archaïques, high tech poussé jusqu'à l'inimaginable et, pour couronner le tout, rencontre de tous ces styles en un seul bâtiment. On peut tout concevoir, tout faire, bref, tout construire: est-ce cela,«l'architectura nova»? Est-ce cela, le style fin-de-siècle qui prévaudra pour le millénaire à venir? Au Japon, le visiteur est continuellement poussé au bout de ses capacités de compréhension. Une des raisons à cela est l'amour des Japonais pour la contradiction. Un précepte de base de la philosophie japonaise est «ceci, et cela aussi»: cérémonie du thé et quartier de loisirs débridés à Tokyo, ascétisme du Bouddhisme, du Shintoïsme et société industrielle hédoniste coexistent. De même, à côté de l'architecture futuriste incontrôlée, la traditionnelle maison japonaise — du moins, à la campagne — archétype sévère, dépourvu de tout ornement.

Racines

La tradition japonaise, porteuse des racines de la société, est un élément-clé dans le puzzle national. Aussi est-il intéressant de jeter un coup d'œil sur l'habitat ancien: c'est une maison de bois brut qui, la plupart du temps, n'a

Model for today: Architecture and philosophy of historic Japan (Kinkakuji Monastery, Golden Pavilion, Kyoto)

Vorbild für heute: Bauten und Philosophie des alten Japan (Kloster Kinkakuji, Goldener Pavillon, Kioto)

Modèle pour l'architecture d'aujourd'hui: bâtiments et philosophie du Japon ancien (monastère Kinkakuji, Pavillon Doré, Kyoto)

finished wood, for the most part lacking doors and windows, instead featuring movable walls with rice paper transparencies instead of glass. With the exception of minute built-in closets and family altars there is nothing more than the »tatami«, the ubiquitous rice-straw mat, to dominate the interior. »The first glimpse of a Japanese house is disappointing; it seems plain, is unpainted, and looks shabby for its lack of paint«, wrote Edward S. Morse[1], one of the first American scholars researching Japan, in 1886. Even at that early date he made the mistake of measuring Japan's ascetic stance against his own conceptions and extravagances, and dismissing it accordingly.

He overlooked the fact that he was dealing with structures that were designed for prayer and meditation, and not beholden to the banal standards of Western everyday life. Morse encountered a Japan that had, with the

haus, das (meistens) keine Fenster oder Türen besitzt, sondern bewegliche Wände mit Papiertransparenten statt Glas. Außer winzigen Einbauschränken und Hausaltären gibt es nichts als die »tatami«, die genormte Reisstrohmatte, die das Interieur beherrscht: »Der erste Blick auf ein japanisches Haus enttäuscht; es wirkt unscheinbar, ist nicht gestrichen, und ohne Farbe wirkt es ärmlich«, schrieb bereits 1886 Edward S. Morse[1], einer der ersten amerikanischen Japanforscher. Er machte schon damals den Fehler, Japans asketische Haltung an eigener Vorstellung und Verschwendung zu messen und entsprechend abzuqualifizieren. Er übersah, daß es sich um Häuser handelte, die für Gebet und Meditation entworfen waren und die sich nicht den banalen Anforderungen des westlichen Alltags stellen mußten. Morse traf ein Japan an, das sich in der Mitte des 19. Jahrhunderts in Folge der sogenannten »mejii«-Reformen nach über zweihundert Jahren selbstauferlegter Isolierung dem Ausland geöffnet hatte. Doch trotz dieser Öffnung blieb das historische Bild Japans erhalten: eine gewachsene, im Kern dörfliche Siedlung aus Holz und Stein.

Auch wenn die »Japaner im Laufe dieses Jahrhunderts ihren Lebensstil verloren haben«[2], auch wenn es dem historischen Wohnhaus (in den Städten) so erging wie dem Bonsai und zur

ni porte ni fenêtre mais des parois mobiles garnies de papier transparent au lieu de verre. A part de minuscules placards aménagés dans les murs et des autels domestiques, on n'y trouve que le «tatami», natte de paille de riz aux dimensions immuables.

«Au premier abord, la maison japonaise est décevante, elle paraît insignifiante et, non peinte, manquant de couleur, semble pauvre», écrit dès 1886 Edward S. Morse[1], un des premiers orientalistes américains qui, à cette époque déjà, commet l'erreur de comparer l'ascétisme japonais à ses propres idées de luxe et de le condamner comme par trop différent. Ce qu'il ne comprit pas, c'était qu'il s'agissait de maisons conçues pour la prière et la méditation, qui n'avaient donc pas à remplir les besoins quotidiens de la vie occidentale. Morse se trouvait alors dans le Japon du milieu du XIX ème siècle qui, à la suite de ce que l'on appela les réformes «mejii», s'ouvrait au monde après deux siècles d'isolement volontaire. Mais, malgré l'ouverture, l'image historique persistait: un habitat qui, bien qu'il se fût étendu, restait profondément villageois, tout en bois et en pierre.

Même si les «Japonais ont perdu leur véritable style de vie au cours de ce siècle»[2], même si la maison traditionnelle (dans les villes) a connu le sort du bonsaï et n'existe plus, dans la maison préfabriquée, qu'en miniature

so-called »mejii« reforms of the mid-19th century, just opened itself to the outside world after 200 years of self-imposed isolation. Nonetheless, despite this opening Japan's historic appearance had remained intact: settlements of wood and stone, grown up over time and village-like in their essence.

Even if the »Japanese have lost their life-style in the course of this century«[2], even if things have gone the way of the »bonsai« for the historic residential structure (in the cities) and degenerated to a miniature – a »tatami« tradition-corner in new prefabricated houses selected out of a catalogue – at its core Japan has remained bound to its roots. Itsuko Hasegawa, the only woman among the Japanese star architects, has put it this way: »Evidently, in their innermost being the Japanese people possess ideals that have developed through their long tradition as a rural society«[3], a statement greatly helpful to an understanding of Japan's present-day architecture. After all, this other tradition has molded it, as well as being an indication that much must be interpreted differently than in the West.

»I compose with light«, states Tadao Ando, as does Le Corbusier. However, the Japanese architect composes from light into darkness[4], turning the European hierarchy upside-down, since according to Far Eastern philo-

Miniatur, zur »tatami«-Traditionsecke im neuen Fertighaus aus dem Katalog, degenerierte, blieb Japan im Kern seinen Wurzeln verpflichtet. Itsuko Hasegawa, die einzige Frau unter den japanischen Architektenstars, formulierte es einmal so: »Offenbar besitzt das japanische Volk in seinem innersten Wesen Ideale, die sich aus der langen Geschichte einer ländlichen Gesellschaft herausgebildet haben.«[3] Diese Aussage hilft, Japans Gegenwartsarchitektur zu verstehen. Denn diese andere Tradition prägt sie, und sie ist Hinweis darauf, daß vieles anders zu interpretieren ist als im Westen.

»Ich komponiere mit Licht«, sagt wie Le Corbusier beispielsweise auch Tadao Ando. Aber er komponiert vom Hellen ins Dunkle,[4] kehrt die europäische Hierarchie um, weil entsprechend fernöstlicher Philosophie im Dunkeln nicht das Böse wohnen kann, wie man es im Westen manchmal gern darstellen möchte.

Japanern ist die Symmetrie als Ausdruck von Macht und Stärke fremd, deswegen kommt sie in ihrer Architektur nicht vor. Sie empfinden auch Übergänge von Räumen nicht als trennend und endgültig, und die laszive Verwendung von durchscheinenden Materialien bis hin zum Lochblech – wie an Projekten von Itsuko Hasegawa, Toyo Ito oder Riken Yamamoto – ist unmittelbarer Ausfluß der

dans le petit coin traditionnel-avec-tatami acheté sur catalogue, le Japon a gardé un attachement profond à ses racines. Itsuko Hasegawa, seule femme parmi ces stars de l'architecture, a dit un jour: «Visiblement, le peuple japonais possède dans son être secret des idéaux qui lui viennent de la longue histoire d'une société rurale.»[3] Cette phrase éclaire considérablement l'architecture contemporaine du Japon et l'existence de cette tradition exige une interprétation débarrassée de nos préjugés occidentaux.

«Je compose avec la lumière» dit, après Le Corbusier, Tadao Ando. Mais il compose du clair à l'obscur[4], dans le sens inverse des Européens, parce que selon la philosophie de l'Extrême-Orient, et contrairement à ce que l'on a tendance à croire en Occident, le mal ne peut séjourner dans l'obscurité.

La symétrie, pour un Japonais, n'est en aucune façon porteuse de force ou de puissance, aussi n'apparaît-elle pas dans leur architecture. Pour eux, les passages entre les différentes pièces ne sont pas des séparations et n'ont pas caractère définitif. L'utilisation nonchalante de matériaux transparents, dont fait partie la tôle perforée des projets de Itsuko Hasegawa, de Toyo Ito ou de Riken Yamamoto, découle directement de la tradition «shoji» des portes coulissantes avec

sophy evil cannot live in the darkness, as is so often depicted in the West. Symmetry, as an expression of power and strength, is also unfamiliar to the Japanese, with the result that it does not appear in their architecture. The Japanese do not perceive transitions from one space to another as separating and final, and the generous use of a range of translucent materials, including even perforated metal panels, as found in the projects of Itsuko Hasegawa, Toyo Ito and Riken Yamamoto, are an immediate outgrowth of the Shoji tradition, with its sliding doors with windows of rice-paper parchment.

Kiko Mozuna and Katsuhiro Ishii address the past in a quite directly readable manner. Mozuna's bizarre creations are like mystery-laden visits to old Buddhist temples from a time in the distant past. Ishii, a sharp exponent of Japanese post-modernism, quite simply imitates old buildings.

»Shoji«-Tradition, der Schiebetüren mit Pergamentpapierfenstern.

Sehr direkt ist die Vergangenheitsbewältigung bei Kiko Mozuna und Katsuhiro Ishii ablesbar. Mozunas bizarre Bauten sind wie geheimnisvolle Besuche in einer fernen, früheren Zeit bei alten Buddhatempeln. Ishii, ein smarter Vertreter des Postmodernismus, imitiert alte Häuser.

Kisho Kurokawa kopiert nicht nur, sondern er verbindet auch. An seinen Museen in Nagoya oder Hiroshima tauchen Gittermuster aus der Edo-Zeit auf, eben jener Periode zwischen 1600 und 1868, in der sich Japan auf sich selbst konzentrierte und sich jedem äußeren Einfluß entzog. Kurokawa interpretiert den »torii« neu, den obligatorischen Torbogen vor jedem Shinto-Schrein. Steile Satteldächer sind Reminiszenzen an das traditionelle japanische Haus — und für unsere Augen Erinnerungen an Aldo Rossi, den bekannten italienischen Ar-

leurs carreaux de papier parchemin. Chez Kiko Mozuna et Katsuhiro Ishii, la maîtrise du passé apparaît très clairement. Les étranges constructions de Mozuna nous ramènent à des temps lointains, dans quelque temple consacré au Bouddha. Ishii, habile représentant du postmodernisme au Japon, imite des maisons anciennes. Kisho Kurokawa ne fait pas que copier, il met en rapport différents styles. On voit apparaître dans les bâtiments des musées qu'il a construits à Nagoya ou à Hiroshima, le thème de la grille qui date de l'époque Edo, cette période, justement, qui va de 1600 à 1868 et au cours de laquelle le Japon se referme sur lui-même et se soustrait à toute influence extérieure. Kurokawa y donne une nouvelle interprétation du «torii», l'inévitable arche qui ouvre sur tout sanctuaire shinto. Les toits ensellés sont des réminiscences de la maison japonaise traditionnelle — pour nous, Européens, ils évoquent

Kisho Kurokawa doesn't merely copy, he creates connections. Lattice patterns from the Edo period, the era between 1600 and 1868 during which Japan concentrated on itself and withdrew from all outside influences, turn up on his museums in Nagoya and Hiroshima. Kurokawa offers a new interpretation of the »torii«, the obligatory archway before every Shinto shrine. Steeply gabled roofs are reminiscences of the traditional Japanese house – and remind us of Aldo Rossi, the renowned Italian architect. This is no accident, rather Kurokawa's intention and the result of the Japanese' being deeply caught up in a fusion of East and West.

Proximity to the West
Following their military defeat in 1945, the Japanese adopted their victors' architectural conceptions. The reconstruction was done entirely under the aegis of the International Style, the functionalist modern age. It is hardly surprising that of all things the Hiroshima Peace Museum, designed by Kenzo Tange, was perceived by the rest of the world as Japan's first piece of »modern« post-war architecture. Kenzo Tange also denoted the reconstruction's conclusion with his buildings for the 1964 Olympics. The museum was a container, suspended similarly to a bridge-restaurant over a motorway; the sports halls were

chitekten. Das ist auch kein Zufall, sondern Kurokawas Absicht und Ausdruck einer tiefen Ost-West-Verstrickung der Japaner.

Nähe zum Westen
1945 übernahmen die Japaner nach der militärischen Niederlage die Architekturauffassungen des Siegers. Der Wiederaufbau stand ganz im Zeichen des Internationalen Stils, der funktionalistischen Moderne. Wenig verwunderlich ist es, daß ausgerechnet ein Friedensmuseum in Hiroshima, von Kenzo Tange entworfen, 1955 als erstes Stück »moderner« Nachkriegsarchitektur in der übrigen Welt wahrgenommen wurde. Kenzo Tange war es auch, der dann 1964 mit seinen Olympia-Bauten den Abschluß des Wiederaufbaus markierte. Das Mu-

Aldo Rossi, le célèbre architecte italien.
Il ne s'agit pas ici d'un hasard mais d'une intention, de la part de Kurokawa. C'est le résultat de l'intime familiarité du Japonais tant avec l'Orient qu'avec l'Occident.

Proximite de l'Ouest
En 1945, après leur défaite militaire, les Japonais adoptèrent les vues architecturales du vainqueur. La reconstruction se fit sous l'égide d'un style international, d'un modernisme fonctionnel. Il est donc peu étonnant qu'un Musée de la Paix, construit à Hiroshima par Kenzo Tange en 1955, fût le premier projet architectural «moderne» à être reconnu par le reste du monde. Ce fut encore Kenzo Tange qui, en 1964, signa, avec ses con-

Schizophrenic eclecticism: Tsukuba Center
(Arata Isozaki, 1983)

Schizophrener Eklektizismus: Tsukuba
Center (Arata Isozaki, 1983)

Eclectisme schizophrénique: Centre
Tsukuba (Arata Isozaki, 1983)

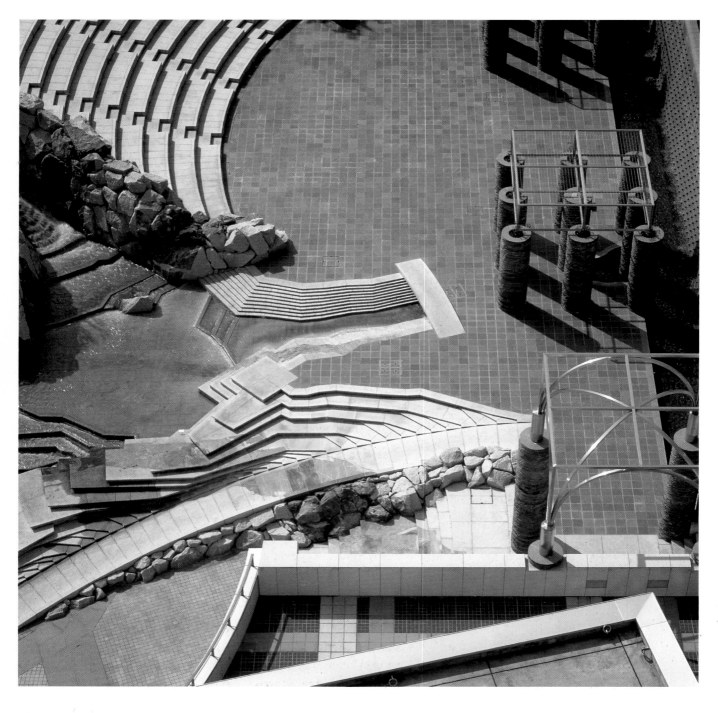

ter, where, according to Isozaki, a »group-photograph of my European colleagues Ledoux, Schinkel, Stirling and Rossi«[7] was created with quotations from European architectural history extending from Roman times to the present.

Up through their supposed »later works«, Arata Isozaki, Fumihiko Maki, Kisho Kurokawa and Kazuo Shinohara have remained conceptual leaders in Japan's architecture scene. With his elegant façades and structural envelopes, Fumihiko Maki can be counted in the modernist camp, an architect who achieves »a condensed portrayal of the modern«.[8] On the other hand, only by appearance is Kazuo Shinohara a modernist architect in the classical sense, since his metallic high tech only looks like high tech, being instead an artificial synthesis of all presently recognized architectural currents. He is, to a certain degree, a »highdeacon of the postmodern«. Certainly Kurokawa and Isozaki have also proceeded in a similarly eclectic manner. Kisho Kurokawa quite openly calls his style »symbiosis«.[9] Isozaki calls his architecture picturesque, which means only that it is pictorial.[10]

At the beginning of the Eighties architects, designers and artists all over the world took their leave from the dictates of one »correct« conception. Permissible was (and is) what-

den, einer, »der eine zusammengedrängte Darstellung der Moderne« leistet.[8] Kazuo Shinohara hingegen ist nur scheinbar ein moderner Architekt im klassischen Sinne, denn sein metallisches High Tech sieht nur aus wie High Tech und ist statt dessen eine künstliche Synthese aller derzeit gültigen Architekturströmungen: gewissermaßen ein »postmodernes High Decon«. Ähnlich eklektizistisch sind sicher auch Kurokawa und Isozaki vorgegangen. Kisho Kurokawa nennt seinen Stil ganz offen »Symbiose«.[9] Isozaki hat sich auf die Vokabel »pittoresk« verlegt; malerisch will er sein, was nichts anderes bedeutet, als daß seine Architektur eine bildhafte ist.[10]

Zu Beginn der achtziger Jahre verabschiedeten sich Architekten, Designer und Künstler in der ganzen Welt vom Diktat einer »einzig richtigen« Auffassung. Erlaubt war und ist, was gefällt und schlüssig ist. Besonders gut damit umgehen konnten Architekten wie Toyo Ito, Kiko Mozuna oder Katsuhiro Ishii, die in den siebziger Jahren »Kritik an der Realität«[11] geübt hatten und weder die heruntergekommene moderne Architektur noch eine wild kopierende Postmoderne als japanischen Weg akzeptieren wollten.

Chaos

In den achtziger Jahren, in Zeiten, als nirgends sonst auf der Welt eine derart prosperierende Wirtschaft so

Isozaki, c'est le mot «pittoresque» qui revient, c'est ce que recherche l'artiste, et cela donne à son style beaucoup de charme.[10]

Au début des années quatre-vingt, des architectes, des designers et des artistes dans le monde entier se soustraient à la tyrannie de la règle absolue. Devient permis ce qui plaît et vous réussit. Des créateurs comme Toyo Ito, Kiko Mozuna ou Katsuhiro Ishii se trouvèrent particulièrement bien de cette liberté, eux qui, dans les années soixante-dix, avaient pratiqué la «critique de la réalité»[11] et ne voulaient pour le Japon ni d'une architecture moderne décadente ni d'un post-modernisme effréné.

Chaos

Dans les années quatre-vingt, à l'époque où nulle part ailleurs dans le monde une économie aussi prospère ne cherchait des investissements comme au Japon, les jeunes architectes connurent leur heure de gloire (voir Katsuhiro Kobayashi, p. 7). On ne cessait de construire, l'amortissement des sommes investies se faisait de plus en plus vite. A Tokyo, 30 000 architectes sont sur le qui-vive, prêts à contribuer à la croissance du Moloch. Dans la ville — et le Japon presque entier est une ville — le mètre carré coûta pendant cette période 150 000 dollars, et parfois bien plus. C'est pourquoi les investisseurs tenaient à

ever might be pleasing or logical. Toyo Ito, Kiko Mozuna and Katsuhiro Ishii were among the architects especially able to work with the new situation. During the Seventies they »criticized reality«[11], and would accept neither the degenerated architecture of modernism nor postmodernism's frenzied duplication as a Japanese approach.

Chaos

During the Eighties, when nowhere else in the world were the calls for investment as loud and persistent as in Japan's prospering economy, the great hour of opportunity struck for these young architects (see also Katsuhiro Kobayashi p. 7). Construction increased steadily, while the amortization periods for invested capital became ever shorter. In Tokyo alone some 30,000 architects stand prepared to expand the Moloch. One square meter in the city centre at times cost US $150,000, frequently even more. This was the main reason investors were ready to afford creative architects, since the ware »architecture« cost less and less in comparison to the real estate itself. Taken together, these factors brought about the »anything goes« attitude in Tokyo and the other major Japanese cities, which gave a green light for the continuation of their unchecked boom.

nachhaltig nach Investitionen schrie wie dort, schlug die große Stunde dieser jungen Architekten (vgl. auch Katsuhiro Kobayashi, S. 7). Immer mehr wurde gebaut, immer kürzer waren die Zeiträume, in denen sich eingesetztes Kapital amortisierte. Allein 30 000 Architekten stehen in Tokio bereit, um den Moloch wachsen zu lassen. Ein Quadratmeter in den Citylagen kostete zeitweise mindestens 150 000 Dollar, oft viel mehr. Das war der wichtigste Grund, weshalb sich Investoren kreative Architekten leisten wollten, denn die Ware »Architektur« kostete im Vergleich zur Immobilie wenig. Dies alles führte zu diesem »Anything goes« in Tokio und den anderen japanischen Großstädten, die scheinbar unkontrolliert vor sich hin »boomen« durften.

Das nun folgende zügellose Wachstum steigerte das, was vor allem Europäern aufgrund ihrer Mentalität und Erziehung schwerfällt, als durchaus sinnvolle Ästhetik anzuerkennen: das Chaos. In Japan ist Chaos letztendlich nichts anderes als ein raffiniertes Ordnungssystem: »In der östlichen Philosophie wohnt im Unvollständigen, im Fragmentarischen und Unausgesprochenen eine größere Kraft als im Vollständigen beziehungsweise Ausgesprochenen. Es fordert ständig unsere Phantasie heraus, und erst unser geistiges Auge fügt es wieder zum Ganzen zusammen.«[12]

faire travailler de véritables créateurs: le coût de l'architecture était bien moindre que celui de l'immobilier. On en arriva à ce fameux «Anything goes» qui régna à Tokyo et dans les autres villes, auxquelles on laissait la liberté d'un boom anarchique.

Cette croissance effrenée exacerba cette notion que les Européens, à cause de leur éducation et de leur philosophie particulières, ont tant de mal à voir comme une notion esthétique: le chaos. Au Japon, le chaos n'est finalement rien d'autre qu'un système particulièrement subtil: «Dans la philosophie orientale l'inachevé, le fragmentaire et l'inexprimé secrètent une force plus grande que l'achevé et l'exprimé. Notre imagination est stimulée par le manque et c'est notre œil spirituel qui complète.»[12]

Architectural export: Japanese Pavilion at
the Expo 1992 in Seville (Tadao Ando)

Architekturexport: Japanischer Pavillon auf
der Expo 1992 in Sevilla (Tadao Ando)

Exportation architecturale: pavillon japonais de l'Expo 1992 à Séville (Tadao Ando)

sified the chaos which, by reasons of their philosophy and upbringing, is particularly difficult for the European to recognize as a wholly meaningful aesthetic. In Japan, chaos is ultimately no less than a refined principle of order. »In Eastern philosophy, greater power resides in the incomplete, fragmentary and unspoken than in the complete or distinct. It continually challenges our imagination, and is not reassembled into a whole until it reaches our mind's eye.«[12]

Chaos became the provider of architectural catchwords, and »dealing with chaos« influences almost all Japanese architects and is a key mainspring of their trade. And very probably the reason everyone else perceives Japanese architecture as »very exotic« can be sought here.

However, at first — around the end of the Seventies — even the Japanese were at a loss concerning how to treat chaos. At the beginning denial and refusal were their primary responses. An architecture of introverted encapsulization arose, the wilderness of the city was excluded. In his early buildings, Tadao Ando kept it out with concrete barricades; Hiroshi Hara constructed buildings-within-buildings, thereby relocating the exterior within doors. However, somewhere around the beginning of the Eighties, as Michael Mönninger describes, »Japan's centrifugal, labyrinthine and additive

Chaos wurde zum entscheidenden Stichwortgeber für Architektur; der »Umgang mit dem Chaos« beeinflußt fast alle japanischen Architekten und ist eine entscheidende Triebfeder ihres Handelns. Und sehr wahrscheinlich ist hier der Grund zu suchen, warum alle anderen die japanische Architektur als »sehr exotisch« empfinden.

Aber auch die Japaner waren zunächst — etwa Ende der siebziger Jahre — ratlos, wie man mit dem Chaos umgehen sollte. Am Anfang stand die Verneinung, die Ablehnung. Eine Architektur der introvertierten Abkapselung entstand, die Stadtwüste wurde ausgeschlossen. Bei frühen Häusern sperrte sie Tadao Ando per Beton aus, Hiroshi Hara baute Häuser ins Haus und verlegte so die Außenwelt komplett nach innen. Doch etwa am Anfang der achtziger Jahre wurden, wie Michael Mönninger schreibt, die »zentrifugalen, labyrinthischen und additiven Stadtstrukturen Japans«[13] zum wichtigen Katalysator. Wie die japanischen Architekten damit umgehen, ist ihre eigentliche Leistung zum Fin de siècle. Sie gingen unterschiedlich vor.

Auf der einen Seite des Spektrums der »Chaoten« stehen die Zerstörer, die allerdings mit ihrer Vorgehensweise durchaus konstruktiv sein wollen. Dazu zählen, quer durch die verschiedenen traditionellen stilistischen Ein-

Le chaos devint le pivot de l'architecture, la «gestion du chaos» est le fait de presque tous les conctructeurs japonais, une de leurs motivations profondes. C'est sans doute la raison pour laquelle on juge l'architecture japonaise «très exotique».

Pourtant, au début, vers la fin des années soixante-dix, les Japonais euxmêmes se demandaient par quel bout le prendre, ce chaos. Ils réagirent d'abord par la négation et le refus. Une architecture introvertie, «encapsulée», naquit et le désert urbain fut repoussé. Les premières maisons de Tadao Ando le maintiennent dehors grâce à des parois de béton. Hiroshi Hara se met à construire des maisons dans la maison et à transférer totalement l'extérieur à l'intérieur. Mais, ·vers le début des années quatre-

urban structure«[13] became a significant creative catalyst. The Japanese architects' handling of this is their true contribution to the fin de siècle. They proceeded in various ways.

On one extreme of the »exponents of chaos« spectrum are the destroyers, who want, of course, to be thoroughly constructive in their approach. Counted among this group, cutting right across the various traditional stylistic classifications, are Shin Takamatsu, Kazuo Shinohara and even the formally reserved Fumihiko Maki: »My Spiral Building symbolizes the image of the city: an environment which offers itself cut into pieces, though it derives its vitality from this very dismemberment.«[14]

The Western visitor is conscious of this chaos primarily through its excess of secondary elements: advertising placards added to an almost indissoluble web of electrical cables, posters and displays. This »empire of signs«[15], as it has been described by philosopher Roland Barthes, is analyzed, alienated, processed and finally assembled in utterly new images.

For Shin Takamatsu they can even assume, as happened with the dental practice Ark in Kyoto, the aggressive lines of a steam locomotive. This is in final analysis indeed something progressive and striving forward. The tower-like factory façade of Takamatsu's Origin III in Kyoto is so brist-

ordnungen, Shin Takamatsu, Kazuo Shinohara und sogar der formal zurückhaltende Fumihiko Maki: »Mein Spiral Building symbolisiert das Bild der Stadt: ein Umfeld, das sich selbst zerstückelt darbietet, doch aus dieser Zerstückelung seine Lebenskraft erhält.«[14]

Der westliche Besucher empfindet das Chaos vor allem wegen des Überangebots an sogenannten Sekundärelementen: Werbetafeln, dazu das fast unlösbare Gespinst der Stromkabel, Plakate, Displays. Dieses »Reich der Zeichen«, wie es der Philosoph Roland Barthes beschrieb,[15] wird von den Architekten analysiert, verfremdet, verarbeitet, schließlich zu ganz neuen Bildern zusammengestellt.

Bei Shin Takamatsu kann dabei schon einmal, wie bei der Zahnarztpraxis Ark in Kioto, die aggressive Linie einer Dampflokomotive entstehen. Das ist in letzter Konsequenz dann doch etwas Progressives, nach vorn Strebendes. Die turmartige Fabrikfassade von Takamatsus Origin III in Kioto ist derart mit scharfkantigen Hellebarden gespickt, daß bei ihrem Anblick die zarte europäische Seele zusammenzuckt: »Shin Takamatsu zeigt sein tiefsitzendes Mißtrauen gegenüber allem Etablierten, er verweigert sich aller humanistischen Wärme und Güte, die sich moderne Demokratien und Humanisten wünschen, was Ar-

vingt, Michael Mönninger put écrire que «les structures urbaines centrifuges, intriquées et pléthoriques du Japon»[13] étaient devenues des catalyseurs importants. C'est la façon dont les architectes japonais s'y prennent pour les apprivoiser qui est leur vraie contribution au style de cette fin de siècle. Ils ne l'ont pas tous fait de la même manière.

A une extrémité du spectre on trouve les destructeurs, qui, cependant, ont des intentions extrêmement constructives. On compte parmi eux Shin Takamatsu, Kazuo Shinohara et un homme au style aussi réservé que Fumihiko Maki qui dit: «Mon Spiral Building porte en lui le symbolisme de la ville: une zone qui se présente de façon morcelée mais qui tient sa force vitale de ce morcellement-même.»[14]

C'est surtout la surabondance des éléments secondaires qui donne au

Stylized urban chaos in the façades: Kirin Plaza, Osaka (Shin Takamatsu, 1986)

Stilisiertes Stadtchaos an den Fassaden: Kirin Plaza, Osaka (Shin Takamatsu, 1986)

Des façades qui affichent le chaos urbain stylisé: Kirin Plaza, Osaka (Shin Takamatsu, 1986)

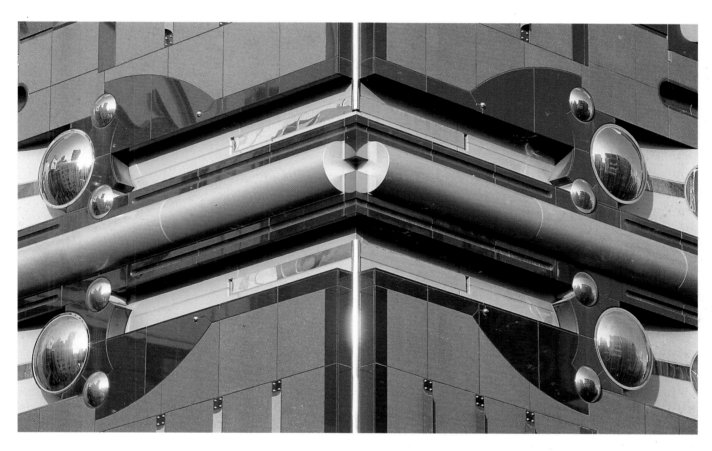

ling with sharp-edged halberds that the tender European soul shrinks at the sight of it. »Shin Takamatsu demonstrates his deep-seated mistrust toward everything established; he rejects the humane warmth and amicability which humanists and the modern democracies wish architecture to express. Instead, his architecture displays death, ritual and Eros.«[16]

With Kazuo Shinohara, who is older, everything turns out more gentle. But, he too is a master of (de)montage; his

chitektur ausdrücken soll. Statt dessen zeigt seine Architektur Tod, Ritual und Eros.«[16]

Bei Kazuo Shinohara, der älter ist, fällt alles eine Spur sanfter aus. Doch auch er ist Meister der (De-)Montage, seine Bauten huldigen der Maschinenkultur, nur haben seine Maschinen keine Aufgaben.[17]

Die Chaosbewältigung funktioniert jedoch im dialektischen Sinne: Einerseits montieren Japaner das Chaos in ihre Fassaden ein, lieben das Frag-

visiteur occidental cette impression de chaos: panneaux publicitaires, lignes électriques, affiches, étalages. Ce «royaume des signes», comme le décrivit le philosophe Roland Barthes[15], est pris en compte par les architectes, analysé, transformé, retravaillé jusqu'à produire un ensemble d'images entièrement nouveau.

Chez Shin Takamatsu, dans son hôpital dentaire Ark de Kyoto, par exemple, cela donne la ligne agressive d'une locomotive à vapeur, qui est

buildings pay homage to the machine culture, though his machines have no task to perform.[17]

The process of coming to grips with chaos certainly operates in a dialectical sense. Thus, on the one hand the Japanese incorporate chaos into their buildings' façades, delighting in the fragment, a playful manner of remaining incomplete, presenting a jumbled diversity of detail through which urban chaos is, as it were, stylized and ennobled. On the other hand, the Japanese use buildings in their totality to keep chaos in check. They construct something along the lines of a walnut shell that will not be submerged in a sea of chaos. Hiroshi Hara, who at first had indeed barricaded chaos from his structures, Toyo Ito and Itsuko

ment, die spielerische Art, unvollständig zu bleiben, bieten eine wirre Vielfalt an Details an, die das Stadtchaos sozusagen in ihrer Architektur stilisieren und adeln. Andererseits konzipieren sie Bauten in ihrer Gesamtheit, um dem Chaos Einhalt zu gebieten. Sie konstruieren so etwas wie eine Walnußschale, die im Chaosmeer nicht untergehen kann. Hiroshi Hara, der zunächst das Chaos aus seinen Gebäuden ausgesperrt hatte, Toyo Ito oder Itsuko Hasegawa gehen dabei getrennte Wege, verfolgen aber ein gemeinsames Ziel: Sie setzen dem Chaos unterschiedliche Metaphern entgegen. Hasegawa orientiert sich an Strukturen und Phänomenen aus der Natur, die in Stahl und Blech nachvollzogen werden. Im Fall von

bien quelque chose de progressiste, quelque chose qui est en marche. Sa façade d'usine en forme de tour de Origin III, à Kyoto, est si hérissée de hallebardes que l'âme tendre des Européens en est toute remuée: «Shin Takamatsu exprime une méfiance profonde de tout ordre établi, il refuse la chaleur et la générosité humanistes que les démocraties souhaiteraient voir exprimées par l'architecture. Au lieu de cela, il montre la mort, les rituels, l'érotisme.»[16]

Chez Kazuo Shinohara les choses sont un peu moins abruptes. Mais luiaussi est un maître du dé-montage; il place ses constructions sous le signe de la machine mais ses machines n'ont rien à produire.[17]

La maîtrise du chaos se fait cependant de façon dialectique. D'une part, les Japonais laissent s'exprimer le chaos dans la façade de leurs créations, expriment leur prédilection pour le fragmentaire, pour la légèreté de l'inachevé, offrent une surabondance de détails qui dramatisent le chaos urbain. D'autre part, le bâtiment dans son ensemble est utilisé pour tenir le chaos en échec. Ce que l'on construit est comme une coquille de noix, qui ne peut sombrer dans la mer du chaos. Hiroshi Hara, Toyo Ito ou Itsuko Hasegawa vont chacun leur chemin mais poursuivent un même but: ils opposent au chaos différentes métaphores. Hasegawa s'inspire des

Hasegawa follow separate paths, although they are in pursuit of a common goal: they set a variety of metaphors against chaos.

Hasegawa is oriented towards natural structures and phenomena: rainbows, trees and mountains duplicated in steel and sheet metal.

In the case of Yamato International, Hiroshi Hara created a little piece of southern Europe — or perhaps more precisely, the ready-made version of a village in the Cyclades.

Conclusions

Thus, as trivial as it may seem, with proximity distant things lose their exoticism. The pseudo-reality of glossy »made in Japan« publications with their splashy architectural reports show only half of the truth. Japanese architecture, experienced and scrutinized in context, proves to be closer to the West, in a figurative sense, than expected, but it is only possible in Japan: on this particular soil, ripened on a substrate of Japanese roots in the stimulating climate of the modern-day megalopolis.

Even for that reason alone, this architecture will not spread around the world without any further ado — even if it represents the first constructed variants of a post-industrial society. However, with the beginning of the 21st century it will play an important role: the exchange of cultures (East

Yamato International hat Hiroshi Hara ein Stück Südeuropa inszeniert, genauer gesagt, die Instant-Ausgabe eines Kykladendorfes.

Folgerungen

Die Ferne verliert also, wie trivial, aus der Nähe betrachtet ihre Exotik. Die Pseudowirklichkeit von Hochglanzgazetten »Made in Japan« mit ihren bunten Architekturreportagen zeigt nur die halbe Wahrheit. Japanische Architektur, im Kontext erlebt und geprüft, beweist: Sie ist dem Westen — im übertragenen Sinne — näher als erwartet, aber sie ist, wie sie ist, nur in Japan möglich: auf einem so spezifischen Humus, der herangereift ist als Substrat aus typisch japanischen Wurzeln, im Reizklima der Megametropolis von heute.

Schon allein deswegen wird sich diese Architektur nicht ohne weiteres über die gesamte Welt verbreiten — auch wenn sie die erste gebaute Variante einer postindustriellen Gesellschaft darstellt. Aber eine sehr wichtige Rolle wird sie zu Beginn des 21. Jahrhunderts spielen: Der Austausch der Kulturen, »East goes West« und andersherum, ist immer stärker geworden. Auch die Vermischung verschiedener Architekturkulturen überrascht nicht mehr in Zeiten, da Japaner in Boston, Wiener in Osaka und Amerikaner in Florenz lernen oder lehren.

structures et des phénomènes naturels: arcs-en-ciel, arbres, montagnes qu'elle reproduit en acier ou en tôle. Pour Yamato International, Hiroshi Hara a mis en scène un petit morceau d'Europe du sud, plus exactement, une version synthétique d'un village des Cyclades.

Conséquences

Et voilà comme, de près, une réalité lointaine perd son exotisme. Les magazines de luxe «made in Japan» montrant une architecture folklorique ne témoignent que d'une demi-vérité. Vue dans son contexte, analysée, l'architecture japonaise s'avère plus proche — au sens figuré — qu'on ne l'aurait cru, mais telle qu'elle est, elle ne peut exister qu'au Japon. C'est son terroir, l'humus où elle plonge ses racines, le climat irritant des métropoles modernes qui la font vivre.

C'est en soi une raison suffisante pour que cette architecture ne puisse facilement se répandre dans le monde; une autre raison étant qu'elle représente la première version construite d'une société postindustrielle. Mais, au début du 21ème siècle, elle aura un rôle très important à jouer : l'échange culturel, «East goes West», et vice-versa, devient primordial. De même, un brassage de diverses inspirations architecturales ne surprend plus, en des temps où des Japonais étudient ou enseignent à Boston, des

Japanese deconstructivism: Angelo Tarlazzi House, Tokyo (Hajime Yatsuka, 1987)

Japanischer Dekonstruktivismus: Angelo-
Tarlazzi-Haus, Tokio (Hajime Yatsuka,
1987)

Déconstructivisme japonais: maison Angelo Tarlazzi, Tokyo (Hajime Yatsuka,
1987)

goes West and vice versa) has steadily gained in vigour. Even a mixture of
various architectural cultures is not
surprising when Japanese study or
teach in Boston, Viennese in Osaka
and Americans in Florence.
This exchange takes place from and in
two directions. Japan is especially experienced in copying other cultures,
ever and again helping itself out of its
own problems with foreign motifs and
methods — even its script derives from
China. The Japanese are masters of

Der Austausch erfolgt aus und in zwei
Richtungen. Japan ist in der Kopie anderer Kulturen — sogar die Schrift
stammt aus China — besonders routi-
niert und hilft sich mit fremden Motiven
und Methoden immer wieder aus
eigenen Nöten heraus. Japaner sind
Meister der Kopie, aber auch der
sanften Veränderung, aus der ein
neues Superprodukt entsteht. In den
fünfziger Jahren haben sie mit Begei-
sterung und Begabung Produkte aus
dem Hause Leitz nachgebaut. Heute

Viennois à Osaka et des Américains à
Florence.
L'échange se fait de et vers ces deux
directions. Le Japon est particulièrement entraîné à copier d'autres cultures — même son écriture lui vient de la
Chine — et parvient souvent à ré-
soudre des problèmes particuliers
grâce à des méthodes ou à des motifs
venus d'ailleurs. Les Japonais sont
des maîtres de la copie mais aussi de
la transformation subtile dont ils sa-
vent faire naître un nouveau super-

replication, and of gentle alteration as well, giving rise to new super-products. During the Fifties they copied products of the Leitz company with great aptitude. Today Nikon, Canon and others export cameras with new qualities and dimensions throughout the world. Things are proceeding similarly with architecture: »Eclecticism, when taken from its better side, is always the mother of a new culture. As concerns architecture, this was already the case for Karl Friedrich Schinkel. When a culture becomes too purist, it dies«, says Kisho Kurokawa. »Thus it must consistently remain open to outside influences, something else we also know through our history. What seems eclectic in my buildings is, in fact, the beginning of a new kind of design procedure in which European and Asiatic influences are blended and a new architecture for the 21st century comes into being.«[18]

In the opposite direction, meanwhile, European and American architects must accelerate this process of amalgamation. If a Mario Botta, who never wanted to work outside of the Swiss canton Ticino becomes a matter of course with his Watari-um gallery in Tokyo, then it must certainly be admitted that Kisho Kurokawa is correct.

The architecture of the 21st century will be global indeed, but it will have little to do with the International Style of the Twenties and Thirties.

exportieren Nikon, Canon und Co. Kameras einer neuen Qualität und Dimension in alle Welt.

So ähnlich funktioniert es auch mit der japanischen Architektur: »Der Eklektizismus, wenn man seine guten Seiten nimmt, ist immer die Mutter einer neuen Kultur. Bezogen auf die Architektur war das schon bei Karl Friedrich Schinkel so. Wenn eine Kultur zu puristisch wird, stirbt sie«, sagt Kisho Kurokawa, »also muß sie sich immer wieder fremder Einflüsse bedienen; auch dies kennen wir aus unserer Geschichte. Was an meinen Bauten eklektisch wirkt, ist der Anfang eines neuartigen Entwurfsvorgehens, bei dem europäische und asiatische Einflüsse gemischt werden und eine neue Architektur für das 21. Jahrhundert entstehen wird.«[18]

In umgekehrter Richtung sind europäische und amerikanische Architekten inzwischen ebenfalls an die Arbeit gegangen, diesen Verschmelzungsprozeß in Japan zu beschleunigen: Wenn ein Mario Botta, der niemals außerhalb des Tessin bauen wollte, plötzlich mit seiner Watari-um-Galerie in Tokio zur Selbstverständlichkeit wird, muß man Kisho Kurokawa ganz bestimmt recht geben.

Die Architektur des 21. Jahrhunderts wird wieder weltumspannend sein. Mit dem Internationalen Stil der zwanziger und dreißiger Jahre wird das nichts zu tun haben.

produit. Dans les années cinquante, ils se sont mis à copier avec savoir-faire et enthousiasme la production de la firme Leitz. Aujourd'hui, Nikon, Canon et Co. exportent dans le monde des appareils de grande qualité et extrêmement performants.

La même chose se passe pour l'architecture: «L'éclectisme, par ses bons côtés, est toujours source de culture nouvelle. Si l'on considère l'architecture, on voit que c'était déjà le cas pour Karl Friedrich Schinkel. Quand une culture devient trop puriste, elle meurt», dit Kisho Kurokawa, «c'est pour cela qu'il faut se laisser pénétrer d'inspiration étrangère, notre histoire nous a appris que c'était une bonne chose. Ce qui semble éclectique dans mes créations, ce sont les prémisses d'une conception nouvelle, où se fait un mélange d'éléments européens et asiatiques et qui suscitera une architecture nouvelle pour le 21ème siècle.»[18]

Face à ce movement, les architectes européens et américains s'emploient à accélérer ce processus de brassage au Japon. Lorsqu'un Mario Botta, qui disait ne jamais vouloir construire hors du Tessin crée sa galerie «Watari-um» à Tokyo, force est de donner raison à Kisho Kurokawa.

L'architecture du 21ème siècle sera à nouveau mondiale et n'aura rien à voir avec le style international des années vingt et des années trente.

1 Edward S. Morse: *Das Haus im Alten Japan*, Papyrus, Hamburg 1983, p. 9. In this volume Morse demonstrates how building construction and architectural culture mirror the philosophy and daily life of historic Japan

2 Quoted from a 1988 conversation with the architect Kazuo Iwamura in Tokyo

3 Itsuko Hasegawa, *Space Design*, April 1985, p. 12

4 See footnote 2

5 This phase of post-war Japanese architecture is closely examined by the critic Hiroyuki Suzuki, published in *Modernes Bauen in Japan*, DVA, Stuttgart 1987

6 Richard Koshalek in: *Arata Isozaki, Architektur 1960–1990*, DVA, Stuttgart 1991, p. 7

7 Quoted from a 1988 interview of Arata Isozaki in Tokyo

8 Charles Jencks: *Die Neuen Modernen*, DVA, Stuttgart 1990, pp. 257–258

9 Quoted from: *Kisho Kurokawa Architecture of Symbiosis*, catalogue for exhibition in Los Angeles, 1987

10 See footnote 6, Hajime Yatsuka, pp. 22–23

11 See footnote 5

12 Gerhard Feldmeyer, »Die Kraft des Widersprüchlichen – Neue Tendenzen in der japanischen Architektur« in: *Bauwelt* 21, 1988, p. 856

13 Michael Mönninger, quoted from various publications in the *Frankfurter Allgemeine Zeitung*, 1992, including »Bilder und Zeiten«, June 20, 1992. Also recommended on this subject is Mönninger's essay in *Japan Design*, Benedikt Taschen Verlag, Cologne 1992

14 Fumihiko Maki, »Spiral« in: *Japan Architect*, March 1987, p. 33

15 Roland Barthes, *Das Reich der Zeichen*, Suhrkamp, Frankfurt am Main, 1981

16 Quoted from a 1988 conversation in Tokyo with Masato Kawamukai

17 Kazuo Shinohara, »Fourth Space« in: *Japan Architect*, September 1986, p. 28

18 Quoted from a 1988 conversation in Tokyo with Kisho Kurokawa

---

1 Edward S. Morse: *Das Haus im Alten Japan*, Papyrus, Hamburg 1983, S. 9. Morse weist in seinem Buch nach, wie Hauskonstruktion und -kultur ein Spiegelbild der Philosophie und des Lebensalltags im alten Japan waren

2 Zitiert nach einem Gespräch mit dem Architekten Kazuo Iwamura 1988 in Tokio

3 Itsuko Hasegawa in: *Space Design*, April 1985, S. 12

4 Vgl. Anmerkung 2

5 Bei dem Kritiker Hiroyuki Suzuki, in: *Modernes Bauen in Japan*, DVA, Stuttgart 1987, sind diese Phasen der japanischen Nachkriegsarchitektur verzeichnet

6 Richard Koshalek in: *Arata Isozaki, Architektur 1960–1990*, DVA, Stuttgart 1991, S. 7

7 Zitiert nach einem Interview mit Arata Isozaki 1988 in Tokio

8 Charles Jencks: *Die Neuen Modernen*, DVA, Stuttgart 1990, S. 257 f.

9 Zitiert nach: *Kisho Kurokawa. Architecture of Symbiosis*, Katalog zur Ausstellung in Los Angeles, 1987

10 Siehe Anm. 6, Hajime Yatsuka, S. 22 f.

11 Vgl. Anm. 5

12 Gerhard Feldmeyer, »Die Kraft des Widersprüchlichen – Neue Tendenzen in der japanischen Architektur«, in: *Bauwelt* 21, 1988, S. 856 ff.

13 Michael Mönninger, zitiert nach diversen Veröffentlichungen in der *Frankfurter Allgemeinen Zeitung* 1992, u. a. »Bilder und Zeiten«, 20. 6. 1992. Empfehlenswert ist in diesem Zusammenhang auch Mönningers Essay in: *Japan Design*, Benedikt Taschen Verlag, Köln 1992

14 Fumihiko Maki, »Spiral« in: *Japan Architect*, März 1987, S. 33

15 Roland Barthes: *Das Reich der Zeichen*, Suhrkamp, Frankfurt/M. 1981

16 Zitiert nach einem Gespräch mit dem Bauhistoriker Masato Kawamukai 1988 in Tokio

17 Kazuo Shinohara, »Fourth Space« in: *Japan Architect*, September 1986, S. 28

18 Zitiert nach einem Gespräch mit Kisho Kurokawa 1988 in Tokio

---

1 Edward S. Morse: *Das Haus im Alten Japan*, Papyrus, Hambourg 1983, p. 9. Morse montre que la construction des maisons et la culture qui s'y rattachait étaient un reflet de la philosophie et de la vie dans le Japon ancien

2 Cité d'après une conversation avec Kazuo Iwamura, à Tokyo, en 1988

3 Itsuko Hasegawa in: *Space Design*, avril 1985, p. 12

4 Voir note (2)

5 Pour le critique Hiroyuki Suzuki, *Modernes Bauen in Japan*, DVA, Stuttgart 1987, ces phases sont reconnaissables dans l'architecture d'après-guerre

6 Richard Koshalek in: *Arata Isozaki, Architektur 1960–1990*, DVA, Stuttgart, 1991, p. 7

7 Cité d'après un interview d'Arata Isozaki, à Tokyo, en 1988

8 Charles Jencks: *Die Neuen Modernen*, DVA, Stuttgart 1990, p. 257 et suir

9 Cité d'après: *Kisho Kurokawa. Architecture of Symbiosis*, catalogue de l'exposition de Los Angeles, 1987

10 Voir note (6), Hajime Yatsuka, p. 22

11 Voir note (5)

12 Gerhard Feldmeyer: «Die Kraft des Widersprüchlichen – Neue Tendenzen in der japanischen Architektur» in: *Bauwelt* 21, 1988, p. 856 et suir

13 Cité d'après divers articles de Michael Mönninger parus dans le quotidien *Frankfurter Allgemeine Zeitung* en 1992, entre autres dans l'édition du 20. 6. 1992 sous la rubrique «Bilder und Zeiten». Nous recommandons de Michael Mönninger un essai paru dans *Japan Design*, éditions Benedikt Taschen, Cologne 1992

14 Fumihiko Maki, «Spiral», in: *Japan Architect*, 1987, p. 33

15 Roland Barthes: *Das Reich der Zeichen*, Suhrkamp, Francfort/M., 1981

16 Cité d'après une conversation avec Masato Kawamukai à Tokyo, en 1988

17 Kazuo Shinohara, «Fourth Space», in: *Japan Architect*, sept. 1986, p. 28

18 Cité d'après une conversation avec Kisho Kurokawa, à Tokyo, en 1988

A new style for the world? Edoken Building, Tokyo (Atsushi Kitagawara, 1990)

Ein neuer Stil für die Welt? Edoken-Haus, Tokio (Atsushi Kitagawara, 1990)

Un style nouveau pour le monde? Maison Edoken, Tokyo (Atsushi Kitagawara, 1990)

45

TADAO ANDO

Tadao Ando (* 1941) combines classical modern architecture with Far Eastern philosophy. He takes his example from »super-father« Le Corbusier, whose work he studied intensively in Europe. In architecture he is an autodidact, but he is a trained boxer. A restless man, who can become loud in contrast to his disciplined, silent architecture, which aspires to be nothing more than »constructed nothingness«. Three things distinguish Ando's buildings: a love of geometry, the longing to incorporate nature into his architecture, and a leaning toward authentic materials, especially concrete. Ando's trademark is his concrete walls' construction grid, measuring 90 x 180 centimeters. Each of these has six holes into which the moulding board screws are driven during construction. Astonishingly frequent the non-Christian Ando creates churches – a special kind of confrontation of East and West.

Tadao Ando (* 1941) verbindet die klassische moderne Architektur mit fernöstlicher Philosophie. Sein Vorbild ist »Übervater« Le Corbusier, dessen Werke er in Europa ausführlich studiert hat. Ando ist Autodidakt, aber gelernter Boxer; ein quirliger Mann, der auch einmal laut wird im Gegensatz zu seiner disziplinierten, leisen Architektur, die nicht mehr als »gebautes Nichts« sein möchte. Drei Dinge bestimmen Andos Bauten: die Liebe zur Geometrie, der Wunsch, Natur in seine Architektur einzubeziehen, und die Neigung zu authentischen Materialien, vor allem Beton. Sein Markenzeichen ist das 90 x 180 cm große Konstruktionsraster seiner Betonwände mit jeweils sechs Löchern, in denen während der Bauzeit die Verschraubungen für die Schalungsbretter stecken. Erstaunlich häufig beschäftigt sich der Nicht-Christ Ando mit dem Kirchenbau – eine besondere Art der Ost-West-Auseinandersetzung.

Le style de Tadao Ando (*1941) se situe à la rencontre de l'architecture moderne classique et de la philosophie de l'Extrême-Orient. Le modèle de l'architecte est Le Corbusier, le «Père Fondateur», dont il connaît bien l'œuvre pour l'avoir étudiée en Europe. Autodidacte de l'architecture mais boxeur professionnel, Ando est un homme exubérant qui, à l'occasion, sait pousser un coup de gueule, alors que ses créations, sobres et maîtrisées, ont l'ambition de n'être que des «riens construits». Trois éléments président aux constructions d'Ando: l'amour de la géométrie, le désir de faire intervenir la nature et sa préférence pour des matériaux authentiques, le béton surtout. Sa signature est la grille de 90 x 180 cm dont les six trous servent à visser les planches du coffrage, pendant la construction. Pour un non-chrétien, Ando construit beaucoup d'églises, c'est sans doute sa façon de se situer dans la confrontation est-ouest.

We need order to give dignity to life.

Wir brauchen Ordnung, um dem Leben Würde zu geben.

Nous avons besoin d'ordre pour donner à la vie toute sa dignité.

TADAO ANDO

Church on the Water, detail

In the sign of the cross: Grid in roof and concrete skeleton (right page) of the structure's upper section; outside, a crucifix is suspended over the water in front of the sanctuary (above); below: freehand sketch

Im Zeichen des Kreuzes: Lichtrasterdecke und Betonskelett (rechte Seite) des oberen Baukörpers; außen vor dem Altarraum schwebt ein Kruzifix über dem Wasser (oben); unten: Skizze

Sous le signe de la croix: plafond-grille lumineux et squelette de béton (page de droite) du bâtiment supérieur; dehors, à hauteur du chœur, un crucifix plane au-dessus de l'eau (en haut); en bas: esquisse

CHURCH ON THE WATER 1988

»It would best suit me to build houses without roofs – then nature would remain palpable,« says Ando. The Church on the Water on the island Hokkaido lives up to his creed. It is composed of two sections, the upper a »Box of Lights«, featuring an open roof and walls consisting of a framework of four concrete crosses. From there one descends through an arched crypt corridor into the actual chapel, the glazed rear wall of which has the effect of making the lake beyond seem part of the sanctuary.

»Am liebsten würde ich Häuser ohne Dächer bauen, dann bliebe die Natur spürbar«, sagt Ando. Die Kirche über dem Wasser auf der Insel Hokkaido wird seinem Credo gerecht. Sie besteht aus zwei Teilen, der obere ist eine »Box of Lights« mit offenem Dach und Wänden aus einem Rahmenwerk mit vier Betonkreuzen. Von dort geht man durch einen bogenförmigen Kryptagang hinunter in den eigentlichen Kapellenraum, dessen verglaste Rückwand den dahinterliegenden See optisch in den Altarraum einbezieht.

«Ce que j'aimerais, c'est construire des maisons sans toit, dans lesquelles la nature resterait présente», dit Ando. «L'Eglise sur l'eau», à Hokkaido, illustre bien cette profession de foi. Elle comprend deux parties, celle du haut est une «boîte à lumière», toit et murs ouverts naissant d'un cloisonnage de quatre croix de béton. De là on descend par une crypte voûtée dans la chapelle proprement dite, dont le mur du fond, en verre, permet au lac qui se trouve derrière d'être visible dans le chœur.

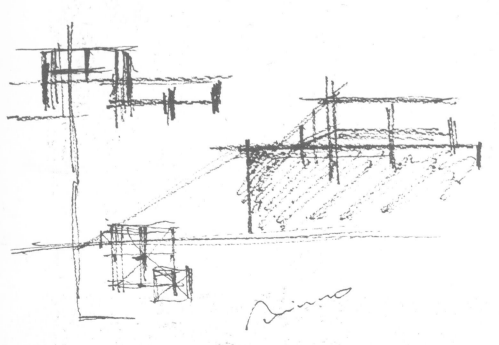

The Church on the Water consists of nothing more than two plain, oversized ashlars. Yet, through its reflection in the water it acquires a quality of melodrama

Die Kirche über dem Wasser besteht nur aus zwei einfachen Quadern. Durch die Spiegelung im Wasser wird sie jedoch zur melodramatischen Inszenierung

«L'Eglise sur l'eau» est faite de deux parallélépipèdes. C'est son reflet dans l'eau qui théâtralise la scène

WATER TEMPLE 1991

This annex to a Buddhist sanctuary on the island of Awaji is sealed in from above by an oval pond with waterlilies. The subterranean temple's entrance is located in the middle of the pond; it leads into darkness. Natural light is only allowed to penetrate at one place. Thus, Tadao Ando tells in his way the story of the »sunken temple«.

Die Erweiterung eines buddhistischen Heiligtums auf der Insel Awaji wurde durch einen ovalen Seerosenteich nach oben verschlossen. Der Zugang zur unterirdischen Tempelhalle liegt mitten im Teich; er führt ins Dunkel. Nur an einer Stelle darf natürliches Licht eindringen. Tadao Ando erzählt so auf seine Weise die Geschichte vom »versunkenen Tempel«.

Sur l'île d'Awaji, Ando a réalisé l'agrandissement d'un sanctuaire bouddhiste qui est clos, au niveau du sol, par un étang ovale planté de nymphéas. L'accès à la partie souterraine du sanctuaire se trouve au milieu de l'étang. On avance dans l'obscurité. A un seul endroit on a permis à la lumière naturelle de pénétrer, créant ainsi une mise en scène mythique pour ce «temple sous' l'eau».

Above surface, a sculpture with a waterlily pond (top); subsurface, a temple between glass blocks (right page); below: sketch

Überirdisch eine Skulptur mit Seerosenbecken (oben), unterirdisch ein Tempel zwischen Glas (rechte Seite); unten: Skizze

A la surface, une sculpture avec un bassin de nymphéas (en haut), sous l'eau, un temple entre verre (page de droite); en bas: esquisse

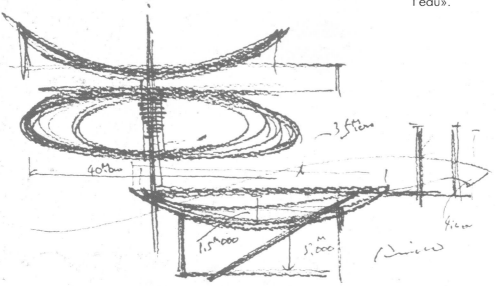

Ando has created an architectural artefact without consuming nature: the temple is situated under water

Ando hat ein Stück Architektur gewonnen, ohne Natur verbraucht zu haben: der Tempel liegt unter Wasser

Ando a réussi une création architecturale sans porter atteinte à la nature: le temple se trouve sous l'eau

RAIKA HEADQUARTERS 1989

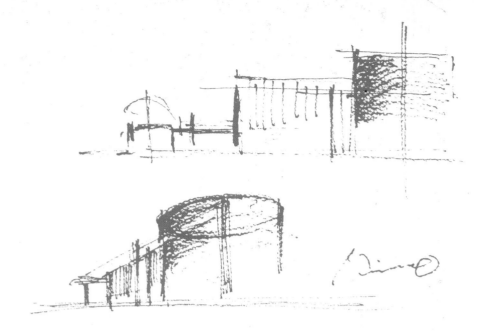

This corporate headquarters in Osaka posed an unusual challenge for Ando. He had to rein in a structure of tremendous scale – 42,000 square meters of usable space. He chose to break up the entire building into individual units, consistently placing each of these under the dictates of a geometric form. Dominant among them is a cylinder for the entrance hall, with a diameter of 40 meters. As a result this office and administrative center does not achieve the intimacy of other Ando buildings.

Für Ando stellte dieses Hauptquartier eines Konzerns in Osaka eine ungewöhnliche Herausforderung dar. Es galt, eine gewaltige Baumasse – 42 000 m² Nutzfläche – zu bändigen. Ando löste das Gesamtbauwerk in Einzelkörper auf und stellte sie jeweils unter das Diktat einer geometrischen Form. Dabei dominiert ein Zylinder für die Eingangshalle. Er hat einen Durchmesser von 40 m, so daß das Büro- und Verwaltungszentrum nicht die Intimität anderer Ando-Bauten erreichen kann.

Avec ce quartier général d'un trust industriel à Osaka, Ando se trouvait confronté à un véritable défi. Il fallait apprivoiser une masse architecturale énorme: 42 000 m² de surface au sol. Le projet total a été morcelé et chaque élément soumis à une forme géométrique différente, tandis que domine un cylindre de 40 m de diamètre abritant le hall d'entrée. Bureaux et espaces administratifs ne possèdent donc pas le caractère intime des autres bâtiments.

Tadao Ando has reduced the structure's massive quality by using walls of glass blocks (left page). The cylindrical unit towers over the entire complex (bottom). It takes in the foyer (below). Above: conceptual sketch

Tadao Ando mindert die Massivität des Bauwerks durch Wände aus Glasbausteinen (linke Seite). Der zylindrische Baukörper überragt die gesamte Anlage (ganz unten), er nimmt das Foyer auf (unten). Oben: Entwurfsskizze

Tadao Ando allège le bâtiment grâce à des murs en blocs de verre (page de gauche). L'élément cylindrique domine l'ensemble (tout en bas). Il abrite le hall d'entrée (en bas). En haut: esquisse

HIROMI **FUJII**

Deconstruction, decomposition, desemiotization – these are the catchwords of Hiromi Fujii (* 1935) when writing on his architectural theories. His buildings have an appearance to match. Time and again he attempts to disrupt entrenched mechanisms of perception, in the process questioning both form and its interpretation in modern and post-modern architecture. In this way he hopes to arrive at new discoveries. Hiromi Fujii is Japan's sympathetic response to the current work of New York's deconstructionist Peter Eisenman. Fujii's buildings are consistently composed of light, grid-based frameworks which appear to have just been shaken out of their rank-and-file order by a light earthquake. Fujii's architecture criticizes society and its firmly entrenched thought patterns – a congenial way of playing the deconstruction game.

Dekonstruktion, Dekomposition, Desemiotisierung – das sind die Schlagworte des Hiromi Fujii (* 1935), wenn er über seine Architekturtheorie schreibt. Entsprechend sehen seine Bauten aus: Immer wieder versucht er, routinierte Wahrnehmungsmechanismen zu stören und dabei die Form und ihre jeweilige Bedeutung, wie sie die moderne und postmoderne Architektur interpretiert, in Frage zu stellen. Mit dieser Methode hofft er, zu neuen Erkenntnissen zu gelangen. Hiromi Fujii ist die kongeniale Antwort Japans auf das aktuelle Werk des New Yorker Dekonstruktivisten Peter Eisenman. Fujiis Häuser bestehen immer aus leichten, rasterförmigen Rahmenwerken, die scheinbar vor einer Minute durch ein leichtes Erdbeben aus der Ordnung geraten sind. Fujii kritisiert mit seiner Architektur die Gesellschaft und ihre eingefahrenen Denkweisen – eine sympathische Spielart der Dekonstruktion.

Déconstruction, décomposition, décodification, tels sont les mots qui reviennent sous la plume de Hiromi Fujii (*1935) lorsqu'il parle de sa conception de l'architecture. Ses créations vont de pair avec le discours. Sans relâche, il cherche à gripper les mécanismes bien huilés de la perception pour mettre en question la forme, et sa signification, telle que la conçoivent l'architecture moderne et post-moderne. Il souhaite ainsi parvenir à une vision nouvelle. Le style de Hiromi Fujii est la version japonaise «douce» du déconstructivisme du New-Yorkais Peter Eisenman. Les maisons de Fujii sont toujours des parallélépipèdes dont la structure légère semble avoir subi dans la minute précédente une légère secousse sismique. L'œuvre de Fujii est une critique des processus mentaux routiniers de notre société, mais son joyeux déconstructivisme a toute notre sympathie.

I want to escape the harmony, consistency and closure of classical architecture.

Ich will der Harmonie, Beständigkeit und Geschlossenheit der klassischen Architektur entgehen.

Je veux échapper à l'harmonie, à la fixité et au verrouillage de l'architecture classique.

HIROMI FUJII

Mizoe House 1, detail

GYMNASIUM 1986

At first glance this gymnasium for the Shibaura Institute of Technology appears no different from an ordinary »functional container«. In reality, however, Fujii proceeded with its design as Chopin would have when composing a piano etude. Basic architectural elements — wall, opening and space — undergo constant transformations and metamorphoses. Thus using unaccustomed harmonies, simple forms like square and rectangle are perceived anew.

Die Sporthalle der technischen Hochschule in Shibaura sieht zunächst nicht anders aus als ein gewöhnlicher Funktionscontainer. Doch in Wirklichkeit ist Fujii beim Entwurf vorgegangen wie Chopin bei der Komposition einer Klavieretüde: architektonische Grundelemente — Wand, Öffnung, Raum — werden ständig variiert und umgewandelt. Einfache Formen wie Quadrat und Rechteck nimmt man wegen des ungewohnten Zusammenklangs neu wahr.

Le gymnase du lycée technique: au premier abord c'est une boîte fonctionnelle. En réalité, Fujii a opéré comme Chopin composant une étude pour piano: les éléments architecturaux de base — murs, ouvertures, espaces intérieurs — sont constamment changés, métamorphosés. Renouvelées par une juxtaposition inhabituelle, des formes simples comme le carré et le rectangle semblent du jamais-vu.

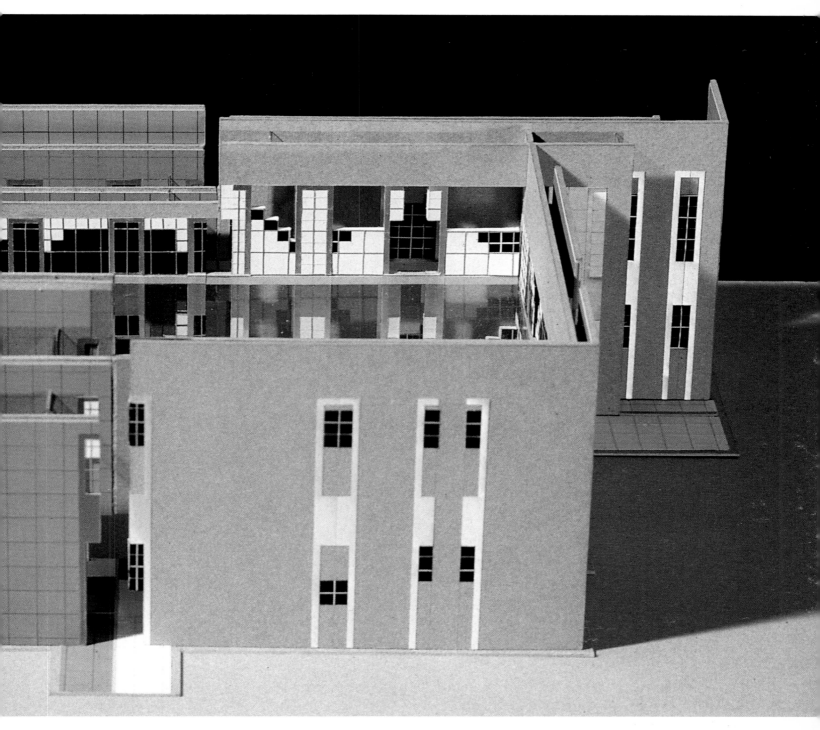

Model of gymnasium (above) and east view (left page): subtle variations of familiar architectural themes

Modell der Sporthalle (oben) und Ansicht von Osten (linke Seite): raffinierte Variationen bekannter architektonischer Themen

Maquette du gymnase (en haut) et vue du côté est (page de gauche): variations subtiles d'un thème architectural connu

MIZOE HOUSE 1 + 2 1988

In the city of Iizuka, Fujii applied his architectural theories to residential houses for the first time. House 1 developed from a rectangular grid. Four L-shaped walls are cut into one another, dissipating the ashlar's austerity. Visitors, on their way from outside to the building's interior, are disconcerted by rapidly changing forms and scales, and thus made to reflect — which is precisely what Fujii intends. House 2, in planning, is an example of an even more progressive decomposition of the familiar grid pattern.

In der Stadt Iizuka wandte Fujii seine Architekturtheorie erstmals auf Wohnhäuser an. Haus 1 entwickelt sich aus einem Rechteckraster. Vier L-förmige Wände werden miteinander verschnitten und lösen den strengen Quader auf. Besucher werden auf dem Weg von außen nach innen durch rasch wechselnde Formen und Größen verunsichert und zum Nachdenken veranlaßt — genau das ist Fujiis Absicht. Das projektierte Haus 2 ist ein Beispiel für eine noch weitergehende Auflösung bekannter Gittermuster.

C'est à Iizuka que Fujii appliqua pour la première fois ses idées en architecture à des maisons d'habitation. La Maison 1 se développe à partir d'une grille rectangulaire. Quatre murs en L se coupent les uns les autres, cassant la rigueur géométrique. Le visiteur, intrigué par des formes et des dimensions sans cesse changeantes, est forcé de réfléchir, ce qui était justement l'intention de l'architecte. Le projet pour la Maison 2 illustre une décomposition plus radicale encore du thème familier de la grille.

Mizoe 1's basic form is a block (top: east elevation, right page: west façade). Mizoe 2 (above) is a more complex continuation of notions applied in Mizoe 1

Die Grundform für Mizoe 1 ist ein Quader (ganz oben: Ostansicht, rechte Seite: Westfassade). Mizoe 2 (oben) ist die komplizierte Fortsetzung von Mizoe 1

La forme de base de Mizoe 1 est le parallélépipède rectangle (tout en haut, vue du côté est, page de droite, façade ouest). Mizoe 2 (en haut) est une variation plus complexe de Mizoe 1

EUROPALIA EXHIBITION 1989

This installation at a Brussels exhibition gave Fujii the opportunity to illustrate his architectural theories beyond the constraints of reality. Metal bars pass in the form of a cube through various stages of metamorphosis, including division, chopping, dissolution and skewing. Fujii varies colours, transforms negative forms into positive ones. The result is a spatial structure which would also be suited to unusual functional requirements.

Eine Ausstellungsinstallation für Brüssel bot Fujii die Chance, seine Architekturtheorie jenseits von Realitätszwängen zu illustrieren. Ein Kubus aus Metallgittern durchläuft verschiedene Stufen der Verwandlung: Sie werden geteilt, zerschnitten, aufgelöst, gekippt. Fujii verändert Farben, transformiert Negativformen in positive. Das Ergebnis ist eine Raumstruktur, die auch ungewöhnlichen Nutzungsansprüchen gerecht würde.

Un stand d'exposition à Bruxelles offrit à Fujii la chance de présenter ses conceptions architecturales sans les contraintes de la réalité. Un cube métallique grillagé passe par diverses phases de transformation: il est divisé, sectionné, dissous, renversé. Fujii modifie les couleurs, change les formes négatives en formes positives. Le résultat est un espace insolite pour utilisation insolite.

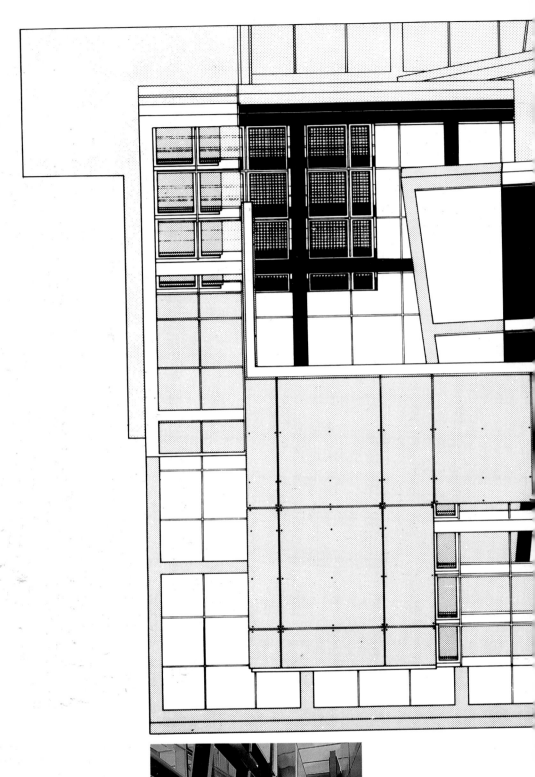

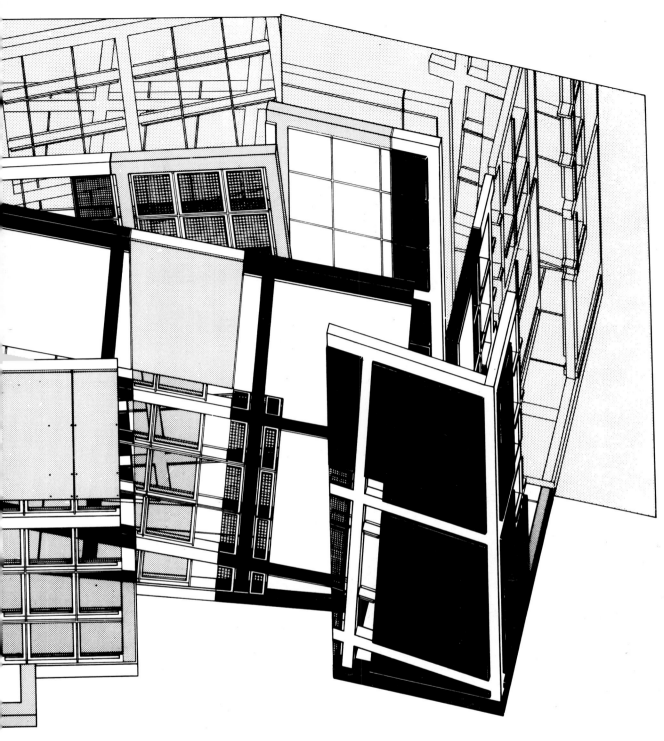

Metal bars in metamorphosis; above: axonometric view of pavilion; left page: detail

Ein Metallgitter wandelt sich; oben: Axonometrie des Pavillons; linke Seite: Detailan-
sicht

Tansformations d'une grille de métal; en
haut, perspective parallèle du pavillon;
page de gauche: vue de détail

HIROSHI HARA

Hiroshi Hara (* 1936) pursues an architecture that defies labelling. It has brought him a singular position in Japan: for Hara, architecture is not a question of style; it rather refers to the laws of nature. He found examples for his conceptions in the natural village structures on the Greek Cyclades or in the tropical forests of South America. Hara considers them the »focus of the universe«.

In detail his architecture is amorphous, occasionally dismembered and perforated. With the play of daylight and changes of season his buildings vary endlessly in contour, hue and overall appearance. Despite his restorationist attitude, Hiroshi Hara is constantly in search of an architecture for the electronic age. He favours high tech materials such as steel and aluminium. He visions buildings that can be raised and lowered, that are in motion.

Hiroshi Hara (* 1936) verfolgt eine Architektur, auf die kein Etikett paßt. Sie hat ihm eine singuläre Stellung in Japan eingebracht: Für Hara ist Architektur keine Stilfrage, sie orientiert sich seiner Meinung nach an Naturgesetzen. Die Vorbilder für seine Konzepte fand er in den ursprünglichen dörflichen Strukturen auf den griechischen Kykladen oder in den Tropenwäldern Südamerikas. Hara hält sie für den »Fokus des Universums«.

Im Detail ist seine Architektur amorph, manchmal zerstückelt und perforiert. Im Wechsel des Tageslichtes und der Jahreszeiten ändern seine Bauwerke immer wieder ihr Profil, die Farbe und ihren Auftritt. Trotz seiner restaurativen Haltung ist Hiroshi Hara stets auf der Suche nach einer Architektur für das »elektronische« Zeitalter. Er bevorzugt High-Tech-Materialien wie Stahl und Aluminium. Seine Vision: Häuser, die auf- und niedergefahren werden, die in Bewegung sind.

Hiroshi Hara (*1936) se livre à une recherche architecturale à laquelle aucune étiquette ne convient. Elle lui vaut au Japon une place très particulière. Pour Hara, l'architecture n'est pas une question de style, elle doit obéir aux lois de la nature. Il tient ses principes des villages primitifs des Cyclades ou des forêts tropicales de l'Amérique du Sud, dont Hara pense qu'elles sont «le point focal de l'univers». Dans le détail, son style est amorphe, parfois fragmenté et perforé. Ses constructions acquièrent, selon les saisons ou les éclairages, des silhouettes, des couleurs et des ambiances nouvelles. Malgré son respect des valeurs du passé, Hiroshi Hara ne cesse de travailler à une architecture pour l'ère «électronique». Il privilégie des matériaux high tech comme l'acier et l'aluminium. Il rêve de maisons montées et descendues, de maisons en mouvement.

I would like my designs to obliterate the borders between nature and architecture.

Ich möchte mit meinem Design die Grenzen zwischen Natur und Architektur verwischen.

Lorsque je construis, je souhaite effacer la frontière entre la nature et l'architecture.

HIROSHI HARA

Yamato Building, window

HARA HOUSE 1974

Hara's own residence, in a little wood in the vicinity of Tokyo, is nearly twenty years old, but it continues to be his »constructed manifesto«: a self-contained universe. Within its confines Hara developed an architecture of the outdoors, featuring cottages and a plaza. The backbone of the structure, which is only 18 meters long, is formed by a staircase of quite the same variety found in many mountain villages, functioning as the central axis of their daily life. Outside one discovers »constructed nature«, like a pile of decaying tree-trunks.

Haras eigenes Haus in einem kleinen Wäldchen in der Nähe Tokios ist knapp 20 Jahre alt, aber immer noch sein gebautes Manifest: ein Universum für sich. Innen entwickelte Hara eine Architektur des Außenraums mit Hütten und einer Piazza. Das Rückgrat des nur 18 m langen Hauses bildet eine Treppe – ganz so, wie sie in vielen Bergdörfern vorkommt und die Lebensachse der jeweiligen Siedlung ist. Außen ist »gebaute Natur« – wie ein Stapel verrottender Baumstämme.

La maison personnelle de Hara, dans un bois des environs de Tokyo, a déjà 20 ans mais elle représente toujours son manifeste architectural. C'est tout un univers. A l'intérieur, on trouve des cabanes et une place de village, toutes choses qui sont normalement à l'extérieur. La colonne vertébrale de la maison, qui n'a pas plus de 18 m de long, est un escalier semblable à ceux qui sont la ligne de vie des villages de montagne. Dehors, ou trouve une «nature construite», un empilement de troncs d'arbres pourrissant, par exemple.

The simple cottage (below left) conceals a
little »village« with alleyways, houses-
within-the-house and plazas (above and
left page)

Die einfache Hütte (unten links) verbirgt ein
kleines »Dorf« mit Gassen, Häusern im
Haus und Plätzen (oben und linke Seite)

Cette simple cabane (en bas, à gauche)
cache un petit «village» avec ses ruelles,
ses maisons dans la maison et ses places
(en haut et page de gauche)

YAMATO INTERNATIONAL BUILDING 1987

In the slipstream of a major road on the inhospitable periphery of Tokyo, the Yamato textile concern constructed a seven-story administration and warehouse building. In the midst of city chaos, where order and serenity are lacking, Hara has reinvented it himself: the building appears like a white village eating its way into the hillside of a Greek island. In its midst are plazas and streets: the administrative building becomes an oasis in a metropolitan desert.

An der unwirtlichen Peripherie Tokios, im Windschatten einer Hochstraße, hat der Textilkonzern Yamato ein siebenstöckiges Verwaltungs- und Lagergebäude errichtet. Wo im Chaos der Metropole Geborgenheit und Ordnung fehlen, erfindet Hara sie: Das Haus wirkt wie ein weißes Dorf, das sich in den Berg einer griechischen Insel frißt. Mitten darin sind Plätze und Straßen: Das Verwaltungsgebäude wird zur Oase in der Stadtwüste.

Dans la banlieue grise de Tokyo, à l'abri d'une autoroute, le trust du textile Yamato a conservé un bâtiment de sept étages, mi-bureaux, mi-entrepôt. Quand, dans le chaos de la grande ville, manquent ordre et douceur de vivre, Hara les invente. L'ensemble fait penser à un de ces blancs villages qui s'accrochent au rocher d'une île grecque. Au milieu, places et rues: les bâtiments administratifs deviennent une oasis dans le désert de la ville.

An administration building becomes a city-within-a-city, featuring gabled roofs, staircases, little temples, streets and atriums (above)

Ein Verwaltungsgebäude wird zur Stadt in der Stadt — mit Giebeln, Treppen, Tempelchen, Straßen und Atrien (oben)

Un bâtiment administratif: une ville dans la ville, avec ses pignons, ses escaliers, ses petits temples, ses rues et ses cours (en haut)

UMEDA CITY 1993

In Hara's view, the high-rise is one of the elemental constituents of the 21st century. His project in Kita, Osaka, is a confrontation between the lean body of a skyscraper and a futuristic Arcadia on its roof. The summit of Hara's high-rise is to be a human paradise towering 200 meters above the ground.

Für Hara gehört das Hochhaus zum elementaren Inventar des 21. Jahrhunderts. Sein Projekt in Kita, Osaka, konfrontiert die schlanken Baukörper eines Hochhauses mit einem futuristischen Arkadien auf dem Dach. Haras Hochhausspitzen sollen menschliche Paradiese in 200 m Höhe über dem Erdboden sein.

Pour Hara, la tour est un des éléments de l'inventaire du 21ème siècle. Celle qu'il projette de construire à Kita, sur l'île d'Osaka, possède à la fois la silhouette élancée typique de la tour et une arcade futuriste sur le toit. Les sommets des tours de Hara se veulent des paradis terrestres, 200 m au-dessus du sol.

The skyscraper of the 21st century: seen from below it presents a familiar sleek façade (above); when examined from the air, it is a differentiated dissolution into small structures (left page)

Das Hochhaus des 21. Jahrhunderts: von unten gesehen, gewohnte glatte Fassaden (oben), aus der Luft betrachtet, eine differenzierte Auflösung in kleine Baukörper (linke Seite)

La tour du 21ème siècle: vue d'en bas, les habituelles façades bien lisses (en haut); la vue aérienne montre la multiplicité des petits bâtiments (page de gauche)

ITSUKO HASEGAWA

Up against the patriarchy within the Japanese architectural avant-garde, Itsuko Hasegawa (* 1941) is the only woman who has managed to achieve recognition. However, her buildings are not meant as feminist statements, even though Hasegawa is conscious of her »outsider« position. Kazuo Shinohara, with whom she collaborated for several years, had some influence on her. This explains her preference for metallic materials. Shinohara has also supported Hasegawa's basic interest in working against the loss of Japanese identity in both city and country. Itsuko Hasegawa recollects the »rural society« that defines Japan at its core. Her buildings are artificial landscapes. Using spheres and pyramids she simulates trees and mountains. She handles materials and forms with a fury comparable to that of Shinohara. Thus she succeeds in designing visions for tomorrow — with motifs from yesterday.

Gegen das Patriarchat innerhalb der japanischen Architekturavantgarde hat sich Itsuko Hasegawa (* 1941) als einzige Frau durchsetzen können. Ihre Bauten sind nicht feministisch gemeint, auch wenn sich Hasegawa ihrer »Außenseiterposition« bewußt ist. Beeinflußt wurde sie von Kazuo Shinohara, mit dem sie mehrere Jahre zusammengearbeitet hat. Das erklärt auch ihre Vorliebe für metallene Baustoffe. Shinohara hat Hasegawa in ihrer grundsätzlichen Haltung bestärkt, architektonisch gegen den Verlust der japanischen Identität in Stadt und Land vorzugehen. Sie besinnt sich auf das, was Japan im Kern bestimmt: die »ländliche Gesellschaft«. Ihre Häuser sind künstliche Landschaften. Mit Kugeln und Pyramiden simuliert sie Berge oder Bäume. Sie geht dabei mit Materialien und Formen ähnlich rabiat um wie Shinohara: So gelingt es ihr, mit Motiven von gestern Visionen für morgen zu entwerfen.

Itsuko Hasegawa (*1941) est la seule femme à avoir pu s'imposer dans l'ambiance patriarchale de l'architecture d'avantgarde japonaise. Ses créations ne portent pas de message féministe, pourtant, Hasegawa est consciente d'être une outsider. Elle admire profondément Kazuo Shinohara, avec qui elle a travaillé pendant de nombreuses années. Cela explique sa préférence pour les matériaux métalliques. Shinohara a encouragé Hasegawa à se battre contre la perte de l'identité japonaise, à la campagne comme à la ville. Elle s'inspire de ce qui fait l'essence du Japon, la «société rurale». Ses maisons sont des paysages artificiels. Au moyen de sphères ou de pyramides elle simule montagnes ou arbres. Elle fait preuve d'autant de violence que Shinohara dans son traitement des formes et des matériaux, parvenant ainsi à créer avec des mofifs d'hier des visions pour demain.

My architecture is meant to create an authentic scene with the use of nature-like symbols.

Meine Architektur soll mit Hilfe von naturähnlichen Symbolen einen authentischen Schauplatz schaffen.

Mon style architectural est destiné à produire un théâtre de l'authentique au moyen de symboles d'ordre naturel.

ITSUKO HASEGAWA

Cona Village, detail

SHONANDAI CENTER 1989

The cultural center in Fujisawa fulfills a variety of tasks. It contains a theater, a community center and facilities for children. Hasegawa wanted a »meeting-place for all the members of society, however different« and created a park resembling a »fairytale village on the moon« (Hajime Yatsuka). The Shonandai Cultural Center is Itsuko Hasegawa's bow to her own origins, the universe, and the ancient landscape of Japan.

Das Kulturzentrum in Fujisawa erfüllt unterschiedliche Aufgaben: Es enthält ein Theater, ein Gemeinschaftszentrum und Einrichtungen für Kinder. Hasegawa wollte einen »Ort der Begegnung für alle noch so unterschiedlichen Mitglieder der Gesellschaft« und schuf einen Park wie ein »Märchendorf auf dem Mond« (Hajime Yatsuka). Das Shonandai Center ist eine Verbeugung Itsuko Hasegawas vor der eigenen Herkunft, vor dem Universum und der japanischen Urlandschaft.

Ce centre culturel situé à Fujisawa remplit diverses fonctions: il comprend un théâtre, un espace communautaire et des installations destinées aux enfants. Hasegawa voulait un «lieu de rencontre pour tous les membres de la société, aussi différents fussent-ils» et créa un parc comme «un village de conte de fées sur la lune» (Hajime Yatsuka). Le Shonandai Center représente, de la part d'Itsuko Hasegawa, un salut traditionnel devant ses propres origines, devant l'univers et le paysage japonais des temps anciens.

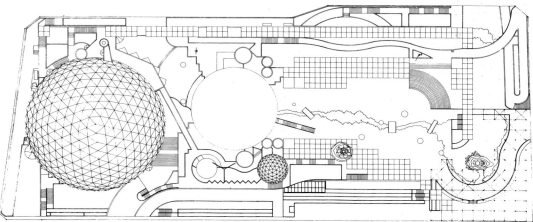

For the cultural center in Fujisawa (see ground plan) Hasegawa selected a pictorial architecture recalling trees (left page), the cosmos and its planets (top)

Für das Kulturzentrum in Fujisawa (vgl. Grundriß) wählte Hasegawa eine Architektur, die an Bäume (linke Seite), an den Kosmos und seine Planeten erinnert (oben)

Pour le centre culturel de Fujisawa (voir plan), Hasegawa choisit une architecture imagée, qui fait référence à la forêt et à l'arbre (page de gauche), au cosmos et à ses planètes (en haut)

Street-front of the Shonandai Cultural Center: Hasegawa composed it of nearly lyrical forms in panels of perforated metal, her favourite material

Straßenwand des Shonandai Kulturzentrums. Hasegawa gliedert sie mit beinahe lyrisch geformtem Lochblech, ihrem Lieblingsmaterial

Façade donnant sur la rue du centre culturel Shonandai. Hasegawa la façonne d'une manière presque lyrique, dans son matériau favori, la tôle perforée

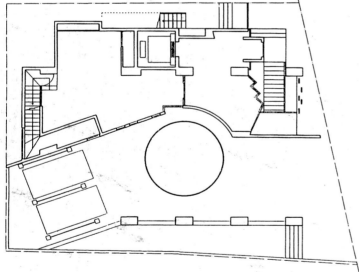

Varied treatment of a building's outer skin is among the standard themes of Japanese architecture: façade of the S.T.M. House (top and right page); above: ground plan

Die differenzierte Behandlung der Außenhaut eines Gebäudes gehört zu den Standardthemen japanischer Baukunst: Fassade des S. T. M.-Hauses (ganz oben und rechte Seite); oben: Grundriß

Le traitement différencié du revêtement extérieur d'une construction fait partie des thèmes typiques de l'architecture japonaise: façade du building S.T.M (tout en haut et page de droite); en haut: plan

S.T.M. HOUSE 1991

Tokyo is Japan's city of unlimited possibilities, also harbouring the dangers of unwelcome, unbridled development. With her S.T.M. House, Hasegawa wanted to come »back to earth«. Thus she fitted the office building in Tokyo with a multilayered façade of glass and metal. It is iridescent depending on the light and the location of the passers-by, taking on the colours of the rainbow. To Hasegawa, the rainbow is a phenomenon closely connected to the Japanese soul: »Architecture is the interpretation of natural phenomena« (Itsuko Hasegawa).

Tokio ist die Stadt der unbegrenzten Möglichkeiten und birgt dadurch auch Gefahren einer unerwünscht maßlosen Entwicklung. Hasegawa wollte mit ihrem S. T. M. House »back to earth«. Sie versah deswegen das Geschäftshaus in Tokio mit einer geschichteten Fassade aus Glas und Metall, die je nach Lichteinfall und Standort der Passanten changiert und Regenbogenfarben annimmt. Der Regenbogen ist für Hasegawa ein Phänomen, das sie eng mit der japanischen Seele verbindet: »Architektur ist die Interpretation von Naturphänomenen« (Itsuko Hasegawa).

Tokyo est une ville où tout est possible, ce qui comporte le danger d'un développement excessif et malencontreux. Avec sa S.T.M. House, Hasegawa a voulu se retrouver «les pieds sur terre». Elle pourvut donc ce grand magasin de Tokyo d'une façade en couches de verre et de métal qui miroite selon l'angle de la lumière et la situation des passants et prend les couleurs de l'arc en ciel. Pour Hasegawa, l'arc en ciel est un phénomène qui est intimement lié à l'âme japonaise. Et, en ses propres termes: «l'architecture est l'interprétation de phénomènes naturels».

CONA VILLAGE 1990

The significant form in the artificial village of Cona is the wave: it laps upon the gently curved roofscape of the complex of nearly 260 units as well as its pronounced balcony grilles and curtain walls. The floor plans of the primarily one-person flats feature movable walls, »prototypes for a new, variable lifestyle« (Itsuko Hasegawa).

Ganz im Zeichen der Welle steht das künstliche Dorf Cona: Sie prägt die sanft geschwungene Dachlandschaft der knapp 260 Wohneinheiten wie auch die markanten Balkongitter oder die Vorhangfassaden. Die Grundrisse der vorwiegend Ein-Personen-Apartments verfügen über bewegliche Wände und sind »Prototypen für einen neuen variablen Lebensstil« (Itsuko Hasegawa).

Créé de toutes pièces, le village de Cona est entièrement placé sous le signe de la vague. C'est cette forme qui imprègne le paysage doucement vallonné des toits des quelques 260 unités d'habitation, tout comme les balcons ou les façades en rideaux. Les plans des appartements, des studios pour la plupart, prévoient des murs mobiles et représentent «le prototype d'un style de vie variable» (Itsuko Hasegawa).

Hasegawa is a master of the gentle transition: façades, staircase parapets and bridges (left page, above) receive transparent walls and sheathing. Right: Cona Village in Amagasaki, amid a typical Japanese urban landscape

Hasegawa ist eine Meisterin des weichen Übergangs: Fassaden und Brücken (linke Seite, oben) erhalten transparente Verkleidungen. Rechts: Cona Village in Amagasaki in typisch japanischer Stadtlandschaft

Hasegawa est la championne des transitions douces: façades et ponts (page de gauche, en haut) sont pourvus de cloisons transparentes. A droite: Cona Village, à Amagasaki, dans un paysage urbain typiquement japonais

KATSUHIRO ISHII

Among the most spectacular buildings of Katsuhiro Ishii (* 1944) is a 1975 structure with 54 different windows. His intention was to do justice to each of the rooms and their functions, as well as to reveal something of each on the façade itself. Since 1980, after his curious gabled highrise in Tokyo — a mixture of Dutch motifs and architecture in the functionalist vein of Louis Sullivan — Ishii is rightly considered as working in the post-modernist direction. However, he was quick to realize that this colourful, ornamental architectural approach was a Western innovation, and thus set about to define a Japanese post-modernism during the 80's, »one that reveals its own spiritual values and thus is connected with tradition« (Kan Izue). The results are collages and modern variations on Japanese architectural traditions. These include the »sukiya« style, which is distinguished by high structural flexibility.

Zu den spektakulärsten Bauten von Katsuhiro Ishii (* 1944) zählte 1975 ein Haus mit 54 verschiedenen Fenstern. Ishii wollte damit den jeweils dahinterliegenden Räumen und Funktionen individuell gerecht werden und an der Fassade davon erzählen. Spätestens 1980, seit seinem kuriosen Giebelhochhaus in Tokio, einer Mischung aus niederländischen Motiven und der Architektur des Funktionalisten Louis Sullivan, wird Ishii mit Recht zur Richtung der Postmoderne gezählt. Schnell erkannte er aber, daß diese bunte ornamentale Architektur eine westliche Erfindung war und verlegte sich in den achtziger Jahren darauf, eine japanische Postmoderne zu definieren, »eine, die sich den eigenen geistigen Werten öffnet und so an die Tradition anknüpft« (Kan Izue). Das Ergebnis: Collagen und moderne Variationen japanischer Bautradition, wie bei »sukiya«, einem Stil mit großer Flexibilität in der Konstruktion.

Une des œuvres les plus spectaculaires de Katsuhiro Ishii (*1944) fut, en 1975, une maison comprenant 54 fenêtres différentes. Il voulait ainsi que la façade reflète la diversité des pièces et des activités qu'elle abritait. Dès 1980, date de son curieux building à pignons de Tokyo, un mélange de style néerlandais et du fonctionnalisme de Louis Sullivan, Ishii est compté, à raison, au nombre des post-modernes. Rapidement, il comprit que cette architecture exubérante était une invention de l'Occident et, dans les années 80, il s'appliqua à définir une post-modernité japonaise, «qui s'ouvre à ses valeurs propres et retrouve ainsi le lien avec la tradition» (Kan Izue). Il en résulte des collages et variations modernes sur le thème d'une architecture japonaise traditionnelle, comme par exemple «sukiya», un style tout de flexibilité.

I want to refurbish the achievements of our architectural history for the present day.

Ich will die Leistungen unserer Baugeschichte für die heutige Zeit aufarbeiten.

Je veux adapter les possibilités de notre histoire de la construction au monde d'aujourd'hui.

KATSUHIRO ISHII

Bunraku, detail of ceiling

SUKIYA-YU RESIDENCE 1989

This residence and guest-house of an industrialist's widow in Okayama is picturesquely situated in a bamboo grove on the Seto inland sea. Hamlet (Japanese: »yu«) is the architect's name for this loose assemblage of a good half-dozen different structures, imitating familiar examples from the »sukiya« tradition and Western architectural history. The daring mixture of such copies renders Sukiya-yu an incomparable ensemble.

Das Wohnhaus und Gästedomizil einer Industriellenwitwe in Okayama am Seto-Binnenmeer liegt malerisch in einem Bambushain. Weiler (japanisch »yu«) nennt der Architekt diese lockere Ansammlung von gut einem halben Dutzend verschiedener Häuser, die bekannten Vorbildern aus der »sukiya«-Tradition und der westlichen Baugeschichte nacheifern. Die mutige Mischung solcher Kopien macht Sukiya-yu zu einem unvergleichlichen Ensemble.

La résidence principale et la maison d'amis d'une veuve d'industriel à Okayama, au bord de la mer de Seto, jouit de l'environnement pittoresque d'une bambouseraie. L'architecte qualifie de hameau («yu» en japonais) ce groupe clairsemé d'une bonne demi-douzaine de maisons différentes qui s'inspirent de célèbres maisons de thé de la tradition «sukiya» et de l'architecture occidentale. L'audace de ce rapprochement fait de Sukiya-yu un ensemble sans pareil.

Da jedes Haus einem anderen historischen Vorbild verpflichtet ist, entsteht eine bewegte Dachlandschaft (unten). Eines der Gästehäuser ist einem Gebäudes aus dem Jahr 1926 nachempfunden (rechte Seite)

Chaque maison s'inspirant d'un modèle historique différent, l'ensemble des toits forme un paysage varié (en bas). L'une des maisons d'amis est la copie d'une construction de 1926 (page de droite).

The Hamlet's Shinto shrine is an allusion to the domes of Richard Buckminster Fuller (left page, top). The architect's declared goal was the achievement of a village-like sense of security (side elevation and below)

Eine Anspielung auf die Kuppeln des Amerikaners Richard Buckminster Fuller ist der Shinto-Schrein des Weilers (linke Seite oben). Dörfliche Geborgenheit zu erreichen war das erklärte Ziel des Architekten (Seitenansicht und unten)

Le sanctuaire shinto du hameau est un clin d'œil aux coupoles de l'Américain Richard Buckminster Fuller (page de gauche, en haut). Le but déclaré de l'architecte était de recréer l'intimité d'un village (vue latérale et d'en bas)

ARATA ISOZAKI

Arata Isozaki (* 1931) is considered the Japanese architect with the greatest degree of worldwide recognition – a cosmopolite who builds between Los Angeles and Osaka, Tokyo and Berlin. It is therefore difficult to get a clear grasp of his position. His teacher Kenzo Tange says of him, »Isozaki has at his disposal not just one, but many vocabularies.« Originally Isozaki was an exponent of Metabolism, then he mused upon geometry as the progenitor of Japanese design. Shortly thereafter he discovered models in Claude-Nicolas Ledoux and Karl Friedrich Schinkel. His simple geometric compositions include the golf club in Oita and the art museum in Gunma. They were followed by Mannerist post-modern structures (Tsukuba city-center). Isozaki's current projects must be seen as a successful synthesis of his thirty years of creative work: picturesque Japanese artworks, with a Western influence.

Arata Isozaki (* 1931) gilt als der japanische Architekt mit dem größten Bekanntheitsgrad weltweit – ein Kosmopolit, der zwischen Los Angeles und Osaka, zwischen Tokio und Berlin baut. Entsprechend schwer ist sein Standort zu fassen: »Isozaki«, so glaubt sein Lehrer Kenzo Tange, »verfügt nicht nur über einen, sondern über viele Wortschätze«. Ursprünglich war Isozaki ein Hauptvertreter des Metabolismus, dann besann er sich auf die Geometrie als Urmutter des japanischen Design, wenig später entdeckte er Ledoux und Schinkel als Vorbilder. Seinen ursprünglich einfach gehaltenen geometrischen Kompositionen wie dem Golfclub in Oita und dem Kunstmuseum in Gunma folgten manieristisch post-moderne Bauten (Stadtzentrum Tsukuba). Isozakis aktuelle Projekte muß man als erfolgreiche Synthese seines dreißigjährigen Schaffens sehen: Pittoreske Kunstwerke aus Japan, westlich beeinflußt.

Arata Isozaki (*1931) passe pour le plus internationalement célèbre des architectes japonais. Ce cosmopolite construit de Los Angeles à Osaka, de Tokyo à Berlin. Il est d'autant plus difficile à cerner: «Isozaki», déclare son maître Kenzo Tange, «n'a pas un vocabulaire architectural à sa disposition, mais plusieurs». Au départ, Isozaki fut le représentant principal du métabolisme, puis il se fit champion de la géométrie en tant que principe fondateur du design japonais, et, peu après, se mit sous la houlette de Ledoux et Schinkel. Ses créations, d'abord simplement géométriques, comme le Golfclub de Oita et le musée d'art de Gunma, évoluèrent vers un maniérisme post-moderne (Tsukuba centre ville). Les réalisations actuelles d'Isozaki apparaissent comme une synthèse réussie de trente années de travail. Ce sont des œuvres japonaises pittoresques dans lesquelles se manifeste l'influence de l'Occident.

The square as well as the circle are the architect's only reliable tools.

Das Quadrat wie auch der Kreis sind die einzig verläßlichen Werkzeuge des Architekten.

Le carré et le cercle sont les seuls outils auxquels l'architecte puisse vraiment se fier.

ARATA ISOZAKI

Disney Building, detail

DISNEY BUILDING 1990

The Disney Corporation's flagship in Orlando, Florida (USA), an administrative building with a total length of 246 meters, resembles an ocean liner. A truncated cone turns into something like an oversized smokestack; it receives the entrance hall. Isozaki employs his signature design approach for Disney, a chest of building-blocks consisting of basic geometric forms, high-tech materials such as glass and aluminium, strong colours and subtle irony – Mickey Mouse ears and duck's bills are found among its inventory.

Das Flaggschiff des Disney-Konzerns in Orlando, Florida (USA), ein Verwaltungsgebäude mit einer Gesamtlänge von 246 m, ähnelt einem Ozeandampfer. Ein Kegelstumpf wird zu einer Art überdimensionalem Schornstein und nimmt die Eingangshalle auf. Isozaki arbeitet für Disney mit seinem typischen Entwurfs-Baukasten aus geometrischen Grundformen, mit High-Tech-Materialien wie Glas und Aluminium, mit kräftigen Farben und feiner Ironie: Mickymausohren und Entenschnäbel gehören zum Inventar.

Le vaisseau amiral du trust Disney à Orlando, en Floride, un bâtiment administratif d'une longueur totale de 246 m, ressemble à un transatlantique. Un cône tronqué devient une cheminée gigantesque et abrite le hall d'entrée. Isozaki apporte chez Disney son habituel jeu de construction fait de formes géométriques primaires. Les matériaux, verre, aluminium, sont high tech, les couleurs sont franches et on perçoit un zeste d'ironie: oreilles de Mickey et becs de canard sont de la partie.

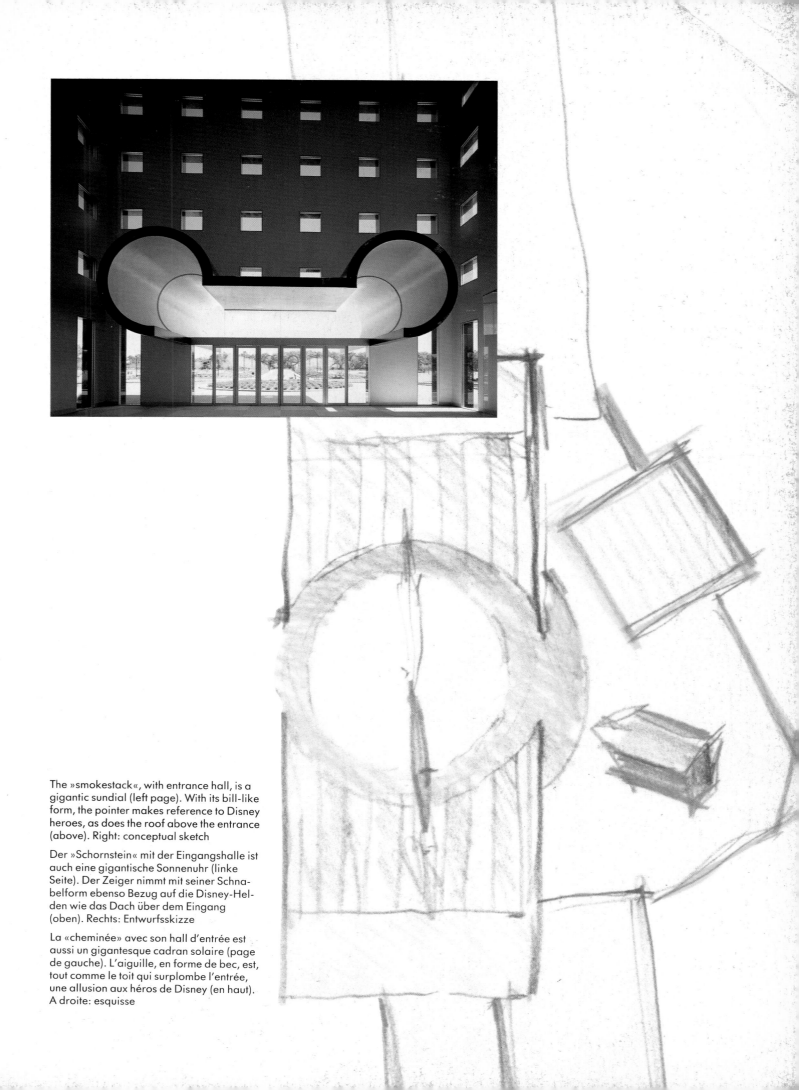

The »smokestack«, with entrance hall, is a
gigantic sundial (left page). With its bill-like
form, the pointer makes reference to Disney
heroes, as does the roof above the entrance
(above). Right: conceptual sketch

Der »Schornstein« mit der Eingangshalle ist
auch eine gigantische Sonnenuhr (linke
Seite). Der Zeiger nimmt mit seiner Schna-
belform ebenso Bezug auf die Disney-Hel-
den wie das Dach über dem Eingang
(oben). Rechts: Entwurfsskizze

La «cheminée» avec son hall d'entrée est
aussi un gigantesque cadran solaire (page
de gauche). L'aiguille, en forme de bec, est,
tout comme le toit qui surplombe l'entrée,
une allusion aux héros de Disney (en haut).
A droite: esquisse

MUSASHI-KYURYO CLUBHOUSE 1987

The Musashi-kyuryo Golf Club is among Isozaki's »rural« projects. It is situated – quite as picturesquely as stones in a Japanese garden – in the Oku-Musashi Nature Preserve. A wooden tower stands at its center. Twenty-meter-tall cedars were brought in on flatcars, rendering the entrance lobby a sort of memorial: »Wood and stone express much of Japan's essence, consecrating the place« (Isozaki).

Der Golfclub Musashi-kyuryo zählt zu den »ländlichen« Projekten Isozakis. Er liegt im Naturpark Oku-Musashi, etwa genauso malerisch wie Steine in einem japanischen Garten. Im Mittelpunkt steht ein hölzerner Turm: 20 m hohe Zedern wurden per Tieflader herbeigeschafft und machen die Eingangslobby zu einer Art Mahnmal: »Holz und Stein drücken viel vom Wesen Japans aus und weihen den Ort« (Isozaki).

Le club-house du golf Musashi-kyuryo compte au nombre des projets «ruraux» de Isozaki. Il est aussi posé dans le parc naturel de Oku-Musashi comme une pierre dans un jardin zen. Au centre s'élève une tour en bois: des cèdres hauts de 20 m, transportés jusqu'ici par camions-remorques, transforment la pièce d'accueil en une sorte de monument commémoratif: «Le bois et la pierre ont beaucoup à dire sur l'âme japonaise; ils font de ce lieu un sanctuaire» (Isozaki).

Water and meadow (left page), wood and stone (above): the golf club fits masterfully into the nature preserve. Below: elevation

Wasser und Wiese (linke Seite), Holz und Stein (oben): Der Golfclub paßt sich gut in den Naturpark ein. Unten: Schnittzeichnung

Eau et prairie (page de gauche), bois et pierre (en haut): le club-house s'intègre dans le parc naturel. En bas: coupe

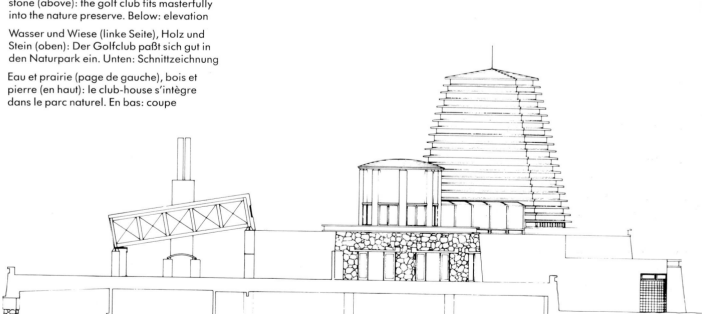

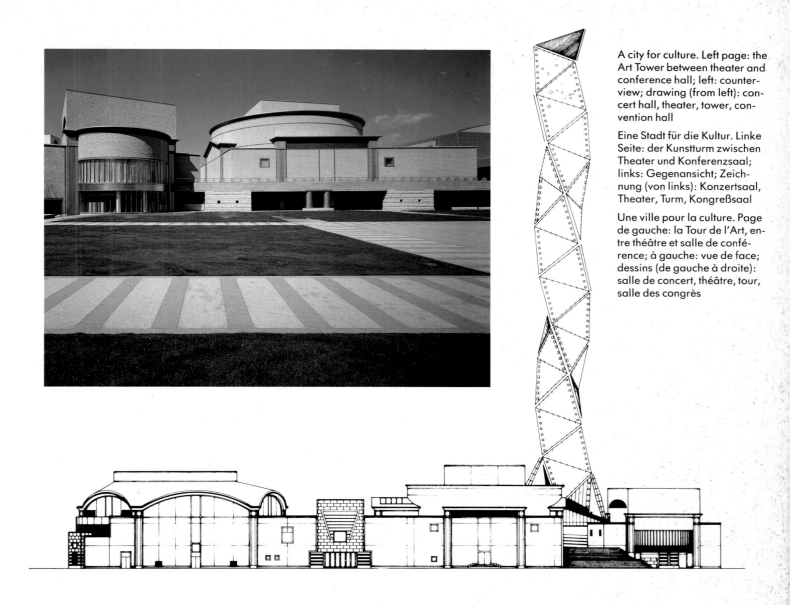

A city for culture. Left page: the Art Tower between theater and conference hall; left: counter-view; drawing (from left): concert hall, theater, tower, convention hall

Eine Stadt für die Kultur. Linke Seite: der Kunstturm zwischen Theater und Konferenzsaal; links: Gegenansicht; Zeichnung (von links): Konzertsaal, Theater, Turm, Kongreßsaal

Une ville pour la culture. Page de gauche: la Tour de l'Art, entre théâtre et salle de conférence; à gauche: vue de face; dessins (de gauche à droite): salle de concert, théâtre, tour, salle des congrès

ART TOWER MITO 1990

This new cultural center was only one among many blocks redeveloped in metropolitan Mito. Isozaki, however, makes a statement of this one: visibly »out of place«, an imposing tower 100 meters in height disrupts an idyll of low blocks for museum, theater and concert hall. The intention is to incite the visitor to think about art and architecture.

Das neue Kulturzentrum war nur eine Blocksanierung unter vielen innerhalb der Großstadt Mito. Doch Isozaki hat ein Zeichen gesetzt und die Idylle aus niedrigen Blocks für Museum, Theater- und Konzertsaal durch einen mächtigen, 100 m hohen Turm gestört, der hier sichtbar »fehl am Platze ist«: Er soll zum Nachdenken über Kunst und Architektur anregen.

Le nouveau centre culturel n'était qu'un ensemble d'immeubles réhabilités parmi d'autres, au centre-ville de Mito. Isozaki a glissé comme un clin d'œil, parmi les immeubles bas du théâtre, du musée et de la salle de concert, une tour de 100 m de haut qui «détonne» franchement et qui est destinée à faire réfléchir le visiteur sur l'art et l'architecture.

Amid its manifold functions Isozaki wished to establish optical leitmotifs: the museum stands under the sign of the pyramid

Bei der Vielzahl der Funktionen etabliert Isozaki optische Leitmotive: Das Museum steht unter dem Zeichen der Pyramide

Isozaki a voulu créer des traits d'unions optiques entre les diverses fonctions du centre: le musée est placé sous le signe de la pyramide

TOYO ITO

As a young architect, Toyo Ito (* 1941) was strongly influenced (as was Itsuko Hasegawa) by his mentor Kazuo Shinohara. Counted among the youthful revolutionaries against the architectural establishment, during the Eighties he found his own direction, an architecture of organic expression, openness and transformation. Thus Toyo Ito finds himself in best company with Japanese architectural tradition, though his designs are for a modern, highly mobile metropolitan clientele. His Nomad Club, a bar in the Tokyo entertainment district of Roppongi (meanwhile also fallen victim to the construction boom), is prototypical Ito, with its open, transparent design. An »oasis for adventurers, who live as they fancy and travel through the cities« (Ito). Inevitably, this preoccupation with nomadic culture brought Ito to the questions of climate, wind and sun. He actively integrates the wind into his architecture.

Als junger Architekt wurde Toyo Ito (* 1941) wie Itsuko Hasegawa stark von seinem Lehrer Kazuo Shinohara geprägt und zählte zu den jungen Revolutionären gegen das Architekturestablishment. In den achtziger Jahren fand er dann seine eigene Richtung: eine Architektur des organischen Ausdrucks, der Offenheit und des Wandels. Toyo Ito befindet sich damit in bester Gesellschaft mit der japanischen Bautradition, aber er entwirft für den modernen mobilen Großstadtmenschen. Sein Nomad Club, eine Bar im Tokioter Amüsierviertel Roppongi, inzwischen schon wieder dem Bauboom geopfert, war mit seinem transparenten Design Itos Prototyp. Eine »Oase für Abenteurer, die nach Lust und Laune leben und durch die Städte reisen« (Ito). Sein Interesse für die Kultur der Nomaden führte Toyo Ito zwangsläufig zur Beschäftigung mit Klima, Wind und Sonne. Er bezieht den Wind aktiv in seine Architektur ein.

Toyo Ito (* 1941) fut, comme Itsuko Hasegawa, fortement marqué au début de sa carrière par son maître Kazuo Shinohara et fit partie des jeunes révolutionnaires en lutte contre l'architecture établie. C'est dans les années quatre-vingt qu'il trouva véritablement sa voie et qu'il acquit un style d'expression organique, d'ouverture et de transformation. Toyo Ito s'y trouve en bonne compagnie, dans la pure tradition japonaise, mais c'est pour l'homme moderne, mobile, des grandes villes qu'il conçoit ses projets. Son Nomad Club, un bar à Roppongi, un quartier chaud de Tokyo, qui a été sacrifé à l'explosion immobilière, était, avec sa structure transparente, un prototype du genre. Une «oasis pour des aventuriers qui vivent selon leur humeur et voyagent de ville en ville» (Ito). S'étant intéressé à la vie des nomades, Ito en arriva à s'intéresser au climat, au vent et au soleil. Et cela au point d'intégrer le vent dans son architecture.

My architecture is a protest against a depraved modern architecture.

Meine Architektur ist Protest gegen eine verkommene moderne Architektur.

Mon architecture est une protestation contre une architecture moderne dévoyée.

TOYO ITO

Nomad Club, ceiling

SAPPORO GUESTHOUSE 1989

This brewery's semicircular guesthouse is embedded in the soil of an extensive park. The majority of its rooms is situated below ground. From outside the structure's only visible portions are the filigreed ventilation turrets and suspended perforated metal gratings. The latter are arranged as sun protection for the arched garden front. The building has become a constituent member of the landscape – as was intended.

Halbkreisförmig gräbt sich das Gästehaus einer Brauerei in den Boden eines weitläufigen Parks. Der überwiegende Teil der Räume liegt unterirdisch. Zu sehen sind die filigranen Entlüftungstürme und schwebenden Lochblechgitter, die sich als Sonnenschutz vor die gewölbte Gartenfront legen. Das Haus wird zum Bestandteil der Topographie – und das war Itos Absicht.

La maison réservée aux hôtes d'une brasserie s'enfonce en demi-cercle dans le sol d'un vaste parc. La plus grand partie de l'espace intérieur est souterrain. On ne voit que les filigranes des tours d'aération et les grilles de tôle perforée, une protection contre le soleil, flottant en bordure du jardin. La maison est devenue élément de la topographie – et c'était bien l'effet recherché.

Three ventilation turrets with striking roofs crown the building (right page). Within, the walls follow the sweep of the hillside (left and floor plan)

Drei Entlüftungstürme mit markanten Dächern krönen das Bauwerk (rechte Seite). Innen orientieren sich die Wände am Schwung des Hanges (links und Grundriß)

Trois tours d'aération très originales couronnent le bâtiment (page de droite). A l'intérieur, les murs suivent la courbe de la pente (à gauche et plan)

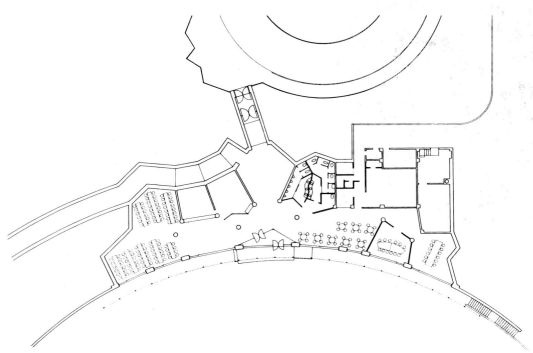

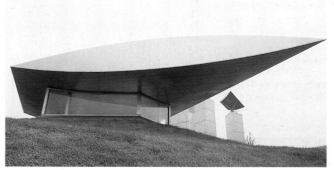

Toyo Ito set this guesthouse into a hillside with great skill. He leaves it to the visitor to answer the question: Which is more important here – nature or architecture?

Toyo Ito hat das Gästehaus sehr geschickt in den Hang gelegt und läßt die Besucher selbst die Frage beantworten, was hier wichtiger ist: die Natur oder die Architektur

Toyo Ito a très habilement accroché cette maison d'hôtes à la pente du terrain. Au visiteur de décider ce qui prime ici, de la nature ou de l'architecture

TOWER OF WINDS 1986
EGG OF WINDS 1989

Both Tower and Egg are sculptures for the new electronic age. The Tower, in Yokohama, is a mechanical structure (ventilation and water tank). With the 1,300 small lamps in its perforated outer skin it becomes a light sculpture, modulated by the direction and strength of the wind. The Egg, in Tokyo, is an »outdoor video gallery« (Toyo Ito) with television screens and exhibition spaces for inhabitants of the »River City«.

Turm und Ei sind beide Skulpturen für das neue elektronische Zeitalter. Der Turm in Yokohama ist ein technisches Bauwerk, ein Ventilations- und Wassertank, der mit 1300 Lämpchen in der perforierten Außenhaut zu einer Lichtskulptur wird, die Windrichtungen und -kräfte sichtbar macht. Das Ei in Tokio ist eine »Outdoor Video Galerie« (Toyo Ito) mit Bildschirmen und Ausstellungsräumen für die Bewohner der »River City«.

Tour et œuf sont deux sculptures de l'ère électronique. La tour de Yokohama est un bâtiment à vocation technique dans lequel sont stockés un système de ventilation et une réserve d'eau. 1300 petites lampes placées dans la carcasse perforée en font une sculpture lumineuse qui indique optiquement la direction et la force des vents. L'œuf, à Tokyo, est une «outdoor video gallery» (Toyo Ito) pourvue d'écrans et de salles d'exposition pour les habitants de «River City».

Environments for the city of tomorrow: the Egg of Winds (above) as »space station« for media and art in a major settlement, the Tower of Winds as a collaboration between wind and electronics

Environments für die Stadt von morgen: das Ei des Windes (oben) als »Raumstation« für Medien und Kunst in einer Großsiedlung; der Turm der Winde als Gemeinschaftswerk aus Wind und Elektronik

Eléments du décor de la ville de demain: l'œuf du vent (en haut), sorte de station spatiale de l'art et des médias dans une cité; la tour des vents, centrale mixte où se rejoignent le vent et l'électronique

KISHO **KUROKAWA**

Kisho Kurokawa (* 1934) began as a radical Metabolist in the Sixties and Seventies. With his »capsule« architecture – minute, but complete living units – piled on top of each other (for example, the Nakagin Capsule Tower, Tokyo), Kurokawa is among the few architects who consistently translate this architectural theory, derived from biological-organic models, into reality. From Metabolism Kurokawa developed his »philosophy of symbiosis« – a »cohabitation« of »space and time«, the »part and the whole« and »past and present«. Taken altogether, Kurokawa's architecture is a spirited synthesis of Far Eastern, predominantly Buddhist (architectural) traditions and currents from modern and post-modern Western movements.

Begonnen hat Kisho Kurokawa (* 1934) in den sechziger und siebziger Jahren als radikaler Metabolist. Mit seiner Architektur der »Kapseln« – winzigen, aber kompletten Wohneinheiten –, die aufeinandergestapelt wurden (z. B. Nakagin Capsule Tower, Tokio), gehört Kurokawa zu den wenigen Architekten, die diese Architekturtheorie, die biologisch-organischen Leitbildern entlehnt ist, konsequent in die Realität umsetzten. Aus dem Metabolismus entwickelte Kurokawa seine »Philosophie der Symbiose« – ein »Zusammenleben« zwischen »Raum und Zeit«, dem »Teil und dem Ganzen« und der »Vergangenheit und der Gegenwart«. Kurokawas Architektur ist eine lebendige Synthese aus fernöstlichen, hauptsächlich buddhistischen (Bau-)Traditionen und Strömungen der westlichen Moderne und Postmoderne.

Kisho Kurokawa (*1934) a débuté dans les années 60 et 70 comme métaboliste radical. Avec ses «capsules», ces unités d'habitation minuscules mais ultra-achevées, posées les unes sur les autres (par exemple Nakagin Capsule Tower, à Tokyo), Kurokawa fait partie de ces rares architectes qui ont mis en pratique les théories basées sur des principes biologico-organiques. A partir de ce métabolisme, Kurokawa se forgea une «philosophie de symbiose», une «vie commune» entre «espace et temps», entre «partie et tout» et «passé et avenir». En résumé, l'architecture de Kurokawa est une synthèse des traditions d'Extrême-Orient, surtout bouddhistes, et des courants de pensée modernes et post-modernes de l'Occident.

Eclecticism is always the mother of a new culture as well.

Der Eklektizismus ist immer auch die Mutter einer neuen Kultur.

L'éclectisme est toujours aussi source de culture nouvelle.

KISHO KUROKAWA

Hiroshima Museum, facade

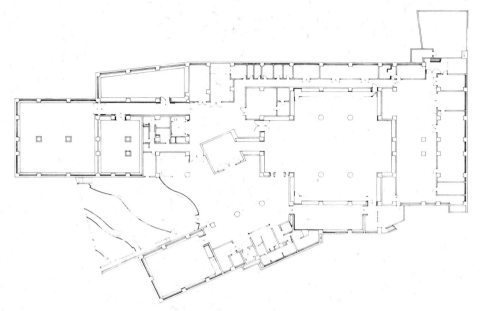

NAGOYA ART MUSEUM 1987

The Nagoya Art Museum is an outstanding example of the »architecture of symbiosis«. The gentle interpenetration of indoors and outdoors – here realized with pergolas, which are also familiar in the West – has its origins in the »ma« philosophy, a complex experience of space and time. The pointed gables and curved glass façades are doubly coded: they bring to mind European architects like Aldo Rossi and James Stirling, though at the same time they are particulars of Japanese architectural history.

Das Kunstmuseum in Nagoya ist ein Paradebeispiel für die »Architektur der Symbiose«. Die sanfte Art der Durchdringung von Außen und Innen – hier umgesetzt durch auch im Westen bekannte Pergolen – entstammt der Philosophie des »ma«, einer komplexen Erfahrung von Raum und Zeit. Die spitzen Giebel und geschwungenen Glasfassaden sind ebenfalls doppelt kodiert: Sie erinnern an europäische Architekten wie Aldo Rossi und James Stirling und sind gleichzeitig Zitate aus Japans Baugeschichte.

Le Musée de Nagoya est l'exemple-type de «l'architecture de symbiose». La douce interpénétration de l'extérieur et de l'intérieur – réalisée ici, comme en Occident, par des pergolas – découle de la philosophie «ma», une vision complexe de l'espace et du temps. Les pignons pointus et les ondulations des façades de verre sont, eux aussi, une double référence qui cite des architectes européens, Aldo Rossi et James Stirling, par exemple, mais se rapporte aussi à des ornements traditionnels de l'architecture japonaise.

The structure's conspicuous, angular form (drawing and above) is an outgrowth of the parcel lines in Shirakawa Park. Right page: front elevation

Die auffällig spitzwinklige Gebäudeform (Zeichnung und oben) ergibt sich aus dem Grundstückszuschnitt im Shirakawa-Park. Rechte Seite: Vorderansicht

Les angles particulièrement aigus des bâtiments (voir dessin et en haut) sont dûs à la forme du terrain de Shirakawa-Park. Page de droite: vue de face.

The Japanophile external structure (left page) with allusions to the »torii«, or archway, is supplanted in the entrance hall by overt quotations from modern European art museums in London and Stuttgart (right page)

Die japanophile Struktur außen (linke Seite) mit Anspielungen auf den »torii«, den Torbogen, weicht in der Eingangshalle offensichtlichen Zitaten aus modernen europäischen Kunstmuseen in London und Stuttgart (rechte Seite)

La structure extérieure typiquement japonaise (page de gauche) et ses références aux «torii» (portails en cintre) laisse la place, dans le hall d'entrée, à d'évidentes références à des musées européens, celui de Londres et de Stuttgart, par exemple (page de droite)

MEMORIAL HALL 1990

This monument, dedicated to the polar researcher Nobu Shirase, was erected in Akita, the prefecture of his birth. Kurokawa used the image of a shelter for survival in ice and snow. A flattened ring some 50 meters in diameter with a conical building of unadorned concrete at its center provides for exhibitions, symposiums, offices, studies, and storage.

Das Denkmal für den Polarforscher Nobu Shirase steht in seiner Geburtspräfektur Akita. Kurokawa gebraucht das Bild eines Schutzhauses, in dem man in Eis und Schnee überleben kann. In einem flachen Ring (Durchmesser etwa 50 m) und einem kegelförmigen Mittelbau aus rohem Beton ist Platz für Ausstellungen, Symposien, Büros und Studienräume.

Le monument dédié à l'explorateur polaire Nobu Shirase se trouve dans sa ville natale d'Akita. Kurokawa utilise l'image d'un refuge qui permet à l'homme de survivre malgré la glace et la neige. Un cercle aplati (50 m de diamètre environ) et une construction de béton brut en forme de quille placée en son centre abritent expositions, congrès, bureaux, chambres d'étudiants et archives.

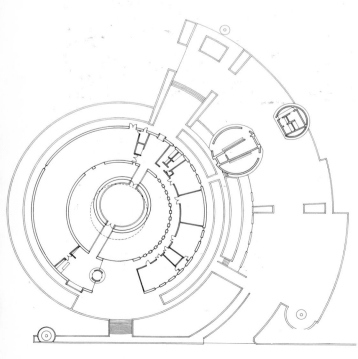

Kurokawa designed this memorial hall, dedicated to a polar researcher, as a free-standing circular building (drawing and above)

Die Erinnerungshalle für einen Polarforscher hat Kurokawa als in sich ruhenden Rundbau entworfen (Zeichnung und oben)

Pour le bâtiment commémoratif dédié à un explorateur polaire, Kurokawa a choisi une forme circulaire qui exprime la sérénité intérieure (voir dessin et en haut)

The entrance (above) and the cone in the center are connected by a narrow passageway (right page, above). A water basin was installed between the outer ring and the inner cone (right page, below)

Der Eingang (oben) und der Kegel in der Mitte werden durch einen schmalen Gang verbunden (rechte Seite oben). Zwischen äußerem Ring und Kegel wurde ein Wasserbecken angelegt (rechte Seite unten)

L'entrée et la quille du centre sont reliés par un étroit couloir (p. de droite, en haut). Entre la circonférence extérieure et la quille, on a aménagé un bassin (page de droite, en bas)

FUMIHIKO MAKI

The stately white buildings of Fumihiko Maki (* 1928) are reminiscent of the »New York Five« in their early phase. As was then true of Charles Gwathmey or Richard Meier, Maki is also counted among the late Modernists, who, bearing today's technical and philosophical knowledge, pick up the thread of the pioneers' achievements in the Twenties. Strictly speaking, Maki should be classified a neo-Modernist, because his thoughts go further. Thus he ties Japanese traditions into his architecture, or with his buildings tries to lend some order to the chaotic urban landscape. For Maki, painstaking detail assumes the role once held by ornamentation, without his becoming a decorator. Maki puts great stock in the power of craftsmanship. Take the Kyoto Museum of Art as an example for such details as the pattern of the floor panels or a banister's trimmings.

Die stattlichen weißen Häuser des Fumihiko Maki (* 1928) erinnern an die »New York Five« in ihrer Frühphase. Wie damals Charles Gwathmey oder Richard Meier zählt auch Maki zu den Spätmodernen, die mit dem technischen und philosophischen Wissen von heute an die Leistung der Pioniere aus den zwanziger Jahren anknüpften. Genaugenommen ist Maki ein Neomoderner, weil er weiterdenkt: So bindet er mit seiner Architektur auch japanische Traditionen ein, oder er versucht, mit seinen Bauten Antworten zur Ordnung der chaotischen Stadtlandschaft zu finden. Das sorgfältig gestaltete Detail übernimmt bei ihm die Rolle des früheren Ornaments, ohne daß er dabei zum Dekorateur wird. Maki glaubt an die Kraft der handwerklichen Leistung. Deswegen muß man zum Beispiel im Kunstmuseum Kioto auf Details wie die Schnittmuster der Fußbodenplatten oder den Abschluß eines Treppengeländers achten.

Les sompteueses maisons blanches de Fumihiko Maki (*1928) rappellent celles des Cinq de New York à leurs débuts. Comme jadis Charles Gwathmey ou Richard Meier, Maki fait partie des «derniers modernes» qui forment le lien entre les connaissances techniques et philosophiques d'aujourd'hui et les réalisations des pionniers des années 20. Très précisément, Maki est un néo-moderne parce qu'il continue de se poser des questions. Il s'efforce de conserver un rôle à la tradition ou, du moins, de restaurer par ses constructions l'ordre perdu dans le chaos urbain moderne. Ce qui était jadis ornement devient chez lui détail soigneusement pensé, sans qu'il s'agisse pour autant de décoration. Maki croit dans l'importance de la belle ouvrage. C'est pourquoi il faut y regarder à deux fois: au Musée de Kyoto, par exemple, l'œil s'accroche à des détails comme la forme des dalles du sol ou la finition d'une rampe d'escalier.

Well-made details are a substitute for the ornamentation of the past.

Gut gemachte Details sind Ersatz für das Ornament von früher.

Des détails soigneusement réalisés remplacent les ornements du passé.

FUMIHIKO MAKI

Spiral Building, detail

Axonometric view (left page): the Spiral Building is a complex web of spaces, ramps, and light. Left: street elevation

Axonometrie (linke Seite): Das Spiral-Haus ist ein komplexes Gespinst aus Räumen, Rampen und Licht. Links: Straßenansicht

Perspective parallèle (page de gauche): la Maison-Spirale est un labyrinthe complexe de pièces, de rampes, de lumière. A gauche: vue depuis la rue

SPIRAL BUILDING 1985

For the front of the Spiral Building, Fumihiko Maki consults the past: the ancient past of Paestum, the historical past of Katsura and, with the cone, the teachings of the Bauhaus. A Japanese corporation had this building, which includes studios, a theater, and conference rooms, constructed for its cultural sponsorship activities. Its rear section is a multilevel semicylindrical atrium, a place for admittance.

An der Front des Spiral-Hauses bemüht Fumihiko Maki die Geschichte: Antikes aus Paestum, Historisches aus Katsura und – mit dem Kegel – die Lehre des Bauhauses. Das Haus ließ ein japanischer Konzern für seine Aktivitäten im Bereich des Kultur-Sponsoring mit Studios, Theater und Konferenzräumen bauen. Im hinteren Bereich besticht ein mehrgeschossiges, halbzylindrisches Atrium, das zur Erschließung dient.

C'est l'histoire de l'architecture qui s'inscrit sur la façade de la Maison-Spirale de Fumihiko Maki: l'Antiquité classique de Paestum, la tradition japonaise de Katsura et, avec le thème de la quille, l'expérience du Bauhaus. Un trust japonais a fait construire cette maison pour y pratiquer le mécénat culturel et l'a fait équiper de studios, d'un théâtre et de salles de conférence. A l'arrière, un atrium hémisphérique, à plusieurs étages, ouvre le bâtiment sur l'extérieur.

TOKYO METROPOLITAN GYMNASIUM 1990

The plot of land in Meiji Park is one of Tokyo's last larger conjoining open spaces. This made possible a generous architectural solution for the multi-use 10,000-seat hall. Maki kept the gymnasium's lines very low and crowned it with a variously folded roof, creating the impression of a gigantic insect.

Das Grundstück im Meiji-Park ist eine der letzten größeren zusammenhängenden Freiflächen Tokios. Deswegen wurde eine großzügige architektonische Lösung für die neue Mehrzweckhalle mit 10 000 Plätzen möglich. Maki hält seine Halle sehr flach und krönt sie mit einem differenziert gefalteten Dach, so daß der Eindruck eines riesigen Insekts entsteht.

Le Meiji Park est un des derniers vrais espaces verts de Tokyo, c'est pourquoi il fut possible de concevoir un projet architectural d'envergure pour une salle polyvalente de 10 000 places. Maki l'a voulue très basse, couronnée d'un toit aux plis irréguliers qui donne à sa construction l'allure d'un gigantesque insecte.

Over a circular floor plan, the roof, in two symmetrical halves, reaches an effective span of 120 meters

Auf einem runden Grundriß entwickelt sich das Dach mit seinen symmetrischen Hälften bis zu einer Spannweite von 120 m

Le toit naît d'un plan circulaire; ses deux moitiés symétriques atteignent une envergure de 120 m

A major portion of the roof's immense load is borne by two arched trusses (above and drawings, right page)

Ein großer Teil der Lasten des gewaltigen Daches wird über zwei bogenförmige Fachwerkbinder abgetragen (oben und Zeichnungen rechte Seite)

Une grande partie du poids de l'énorme toit est portée par deux poutres boutisses de bois cintré (en haut et dessin, page de droite)

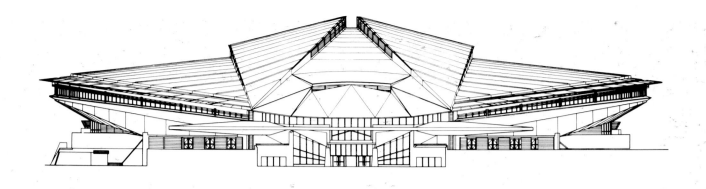

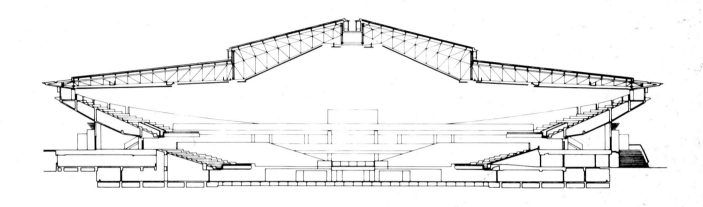

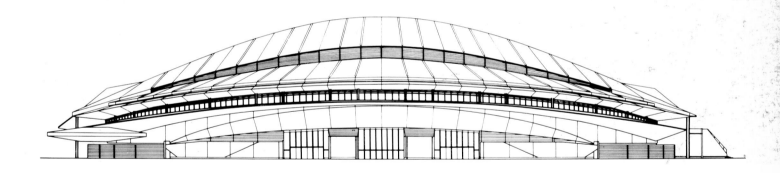

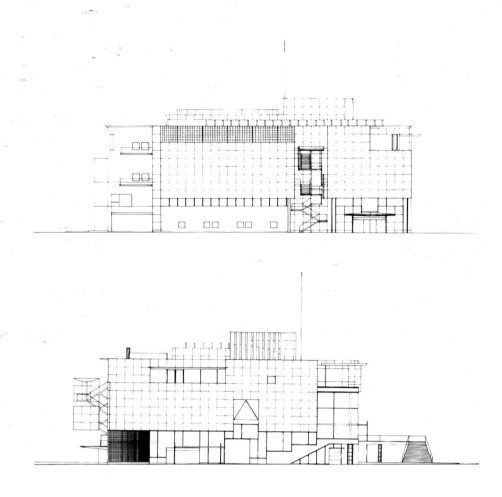

TEPIA BUILDING 1989

TEPIA is the short term of »Techno-logy-Utopia«. The building, located in Meiji Park (Tokyo), features spaces for the use of high technology fairs and exhibitions. The construction materials utilized were selected accordingly: high-tech glazing, aluminium panels, and solar collectors for the roof. For Maki the TEPIA is a »testimony of Japanese industrial society«.

TEPIA ist das Kurzwort für »Technolo-gie-Utopia«. Das Gebäude im Meiji-Park (Tokio) hält Flächen für High-Tech-Messen und -Ausstellungen bereit. Entsprechend war die Auswahl der verwendeten Baumaterialien: High-Tech-Gläser, Aluminiumpaneele und Solarkollektoren für das Dach. Für Maki ist TEPIA »ein Zeugnis der japanischen Industrie-gesellschaft«.

TEPIA est le raccourci de «Techno-logy Utopia». Le bâtiment, qui s'élève à Meiji Park (Tokyo), est destiné à accueillir des foires-expositions High Tech. Les matériaux choisis sont en rapport avec sa vocation: diverses sortes de verre high tech, panneaux d'aluminium et pour le toit, des capteurs solaires. Pour Maki, TEPIA est «un témoignage de la société indus-trielle japonaise».

Both drafted and actual views reveal a
meticulous breaking-up of the façade, an
approach resembling that favoured by
Dutch De Stijl architects

Gezeichnete und reale Ansichten zeigen
eine akkurate Fassadenaufteilung, wie sie
die niederländischen De-Stijl-Architekten
favorisierten

Un dessin et une photographie montrent la
façade à sections, à la manière des architectes néerlandais de l'école De Stijl

KIKO MOZUNA

Kiko Mozuna (* 1941) paraphrases his architecture with an oxymoronic expression of his own invention: »Future Baroque«. He hovers amid styles of every description, between quotations of the past and incantations of the future. He grants himself the freedom to design a country inn as if it were intended to serve as the backdrop for a science-fiction film, while at the same time building museums whose archaic forms radiate such peace and balance as if they had been constructed for eternity. The »Earth« gallery summarizes Monzuna's dialectic: a futuristic metal egg is suspended in a glass container over mystery-laden catacombs and the replica of a historical tea-house. He thus establishes a link »between heaven and earth«. His manifold temperament and style has brought Mozuna close to post-modernism. But he is more than that. He has designated himself as Japan's first esoteric architect.

Kiko Mozuna (* 1941) umschreibt seine Architektur mit der von ihm erfundenen Nonsense-Vokabel »Zukunftsbarock«. Denn Mozuna schwebt zwischen allen Stilen, zwischen Vergangenheitszitaten und Zukunftsbeschwörungen. Er nimmt sich auf der einen Seite die Freiheit heraus, ein Landhotel wie die Kulisse aus einem Science-fiction-Film zu gestalten und gleichzeitig Museen zu bauen, deren archaische Formen Ruhe und Ausgeglichenheit ausstrahlen, als seien sie für die Ewigkeit gebaut. Die Galerie »Earth« faßt Mozunas Dialektik zusammen: In einem Glascontainer schwebt über geheimnisvollen Katakomben und dem Nachbau eines historischen Teehauses ein futuristisches Metallei. So spannt er den Bogen »zwischen Himmel und Erde«. Derlei Stilvielfalt rückt Mozuna in die Nähe des Postmodernismus. Doch er ist mehr: Er bezeichnet sich als den ersten esoterischen Architekten in Japan.

Kiko Mozuna (*1941) décrit son architecture, en une expression qu'il a imaginée lui-même, comme un «Baroque du futur». En effet, Mozuna voltige entre tous les styles, de références au passé en incantations à l'avenir. D'un côté, il se sent la liberté de créer un hôtel de campagne qui ressemble à un décor de science-fiction et de l'autre, de construire des musées dont la structure archaïque sereine donne l'impression qu'ils sont bâtis pour l'éternité. La galerie «Earth» illustre ainsi la dialectique de Mozuna: dans un container de verre un œuf futuriste en métal se balance au-dessus de mystérieuses catacombes et la reconstitution d'une maison de thé. Ainsi l'artiste jette-t-il un pont «entre ciel et terre». Ce sont ces changements d'humeur et de style qui le rapprochent des post-modernes. Mais Kiko Mozuna est plus que cela: il se définit lui-même comme le premier architecte ésotérique du Japon.

My buildings are holograms of the spirit.

Meine Gebäude sind Hologramme des Geistes.

Mes constructions sont des hologrammes de l'esprit.

KIKO MOZUNA

Kushiro City Museum, detail

MONZEN FAMILY INN 1991

This family-operated inn, in Houshi-gun on the island of Ishikawa, consists of a loosely assembled multitude of individual structures. The element lending them order and unity is a gently curving covered footbridge. Arranged along one side are the guest-houses – single-storey cottages – on the other are restaurant and office, the contours of which call a fire station to mind.

Das Familienhotel in Houshi-gun auf der Insel Ishikawa besteht aus einer locker zusammengewürfelten Schar von Einzelbauten. Ordnungs- und Erschließungselement ist ein sanft gebogener, überdachter Laufsteg. An einer Seite liegen die Gästehäuser – eingeschossige Hütten –, auf der anderen Restaurant und Büro. Ihre Kontur erinnert an eine Feuerwehr- oder Bergstation.

Cet hôtel familial situé à Houshi-gun sur l'île d'Ishikawa se compose d'une foule de petits bâtiments jetés là comme une poignée de dés. L'élément organisateur et celui aussi qui ouvre sur l'extérieur est un chemin serpentant doucement. D'un côté, les maisons des visiteurs, petites cabanes de plain-pied, et de l'autre côté, restaurant et bureau, dont l'allure rappelle celle d'une caserne de pompiers ou d'un poste de secours de montagne.

A covered walkway ends as a »flying saucer« (left page). Located to its right is the restaurant (sectional view and left)

Ein gedeckter Fußgängersteg endet als »fliegende Untertasse« (linke Seite). Rechts davon das Restaurant (Schnitt und links)

Un chemin couvert s'achève en «soucoupe volante» (page de gauche). A sa droite le restaurant (schéma en coupe et à gauche)

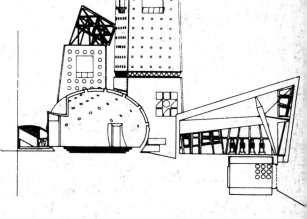

The small guest-houses of this country inn
are based on traditional rural hospices:
Spartan rooms furnished with nothing more
than »tatami« rice-straw mats — shoes off at
the entrance!

Die kleinen Gästehäuser des Landhotels
orientieren sich an traditionellen Landher-
bergen: karge Räume, eingerichtet nur mit
der Reisstrohmatte »tatami«; Schuhe am
Eingang ausziehen!

Les petites maisons des visiteurs de cet no-
tel de campagne s'inspirent des auberges
traditionnelles: pièces nues, seulement
adoucies de tapis de paille, les «tatami».
On ôte ses chaussures en entrant!

The semblance of a »cult-citadel« (right) is the product of a painstaking geometric overlapping of curves and rectangles (left page). Below: Mozuna draws visions of his projects like a »mandala«, a religious visual enigma

Der Anschein einer »Kultburg« (rechts) ist der Überschneidung von Kurven und Rechtecken in akkurater Geometrie zu verdanken (linke Seite). Unten: Wie ein »mandala«, ein spirituell religiöses Bildrätsel, zeichnet Mozuna Visionen seiner Projekte

Le musée doit cet aspect de lieu cultuel (à droite) à l'entrecroisement des courbes et des angles en une géométrie d'une grande précision (page de gauche). En bas: Mozuna conçoit ses projets comme des «mandala», ces énigmes en image, à caractère spirituel ou religieux

KUSHIRO CITY MUSEUM 1984

This museum, perched on a treeless height above the city of Kushiro, is like a monument to cultures of the past with its terraced pyramids intersecting one another and encircling an arched Art Deco central building. The museum derives its magic from both its mystic form – and the uncanny evening light of this northern island.

Auf einer kahlen Anhöhe über der Stadt Kushiro liegt das Museum – wie ein Denkmal für vergangene Kulturen: abgestufte und miteinander verschnittene Pyramiden umfassen einen bogenförmigen Art-deco-Mittelbau. Seine Magie bezieht der Museumsbau aus der mystischen Form – und dem ungeheuerlichen Abendlicht der Nordinsel.

Le musée est situé sur une colline aride, au-dessus de la ville de Kushiro et apparaît comme un monument élevé à la mémoire des cultures disparues. Des pyramides en gradins qui s'entrecroisent entourent un bâtiment central de style Art Déco. L'ensemble tient sa magie de la connotation mystique et de l'extraordinaire lumière vespérale de cette île du nord.

UNOKI ELEMENTARY SCHOOL 1988

Elementary students in Wakami-City can feel as well-sheltered as if they were in an African kraal. But there's even more: Mozuna compares the school with a tree. It is supposed to remind one of roots, climate and history while simultaneously pointing upward like a tree, that is, pointing into the future.

Mozuna firmly repudiates the norm in Japanese school buildings. Behind curved walls of Akita cedars he creates space for yoga and computers: future baroque!

Geborgen wie in einem afrikanischen Kral können sich Grundschüler in Wakami-City fühlen. Aber mehr noch: Mozuna vergleicht die Schule mit einem Baum. Sie soll an die Wurzeln, an Klima und Geschichte erinnern und gleichzeitig wie ein Baum nach oben, das heißt in die Zukunft weisen.

Mozuna erteilt dem Normschulbau, wie er auch in Japan üblich ist, eine klare Absage. Hinter geschwungenen Wänden aus Akita-Zedern schafft er Raum für Yoga und Computer: Zukunftsbarock!

Les enfants de l'école primaire de Wakami-City doivent se sentir aussi en sécurité que des petits Africains dans leur kraal. Mozuna va plus loin encore: il compare cette école à un arbre. Ses racines doivent garder présent le souvenir du climat, de l'histoire tout comme la partie aérienne de l'arbre dirigée vers le haut, vers l'avenir.

Mozuna se déclare contre la conception habituelle de l'école, telle qu'elle existe aussi au Japon. Derrière des murs aux courbes douces en cèdre d'Akita il crée un espace pour la pratique du yoga et de l'informatique: c'est le Baroque du futur!

The school consists of the oval classroom building (the »mental training facility«) and a gymnasium (the »physical training facility«; above left). The broad eaves (right page) are unmistakable references to ancient Japan. Below left: spaces »light, round and complete, like baroque music« (Mozuna)

Die Schule besteht aus dem ovalen Klassengebäude (»die geistige Trainingsanlage«) und einer Turnhalle (dem »Physical Trainingscenter«; links oben). Die weit überstehenden Dächer (rechte Seite) sind eindeutige Referenzen an das alte Japan. Links unten: Räume »leicht, rund und geschlossen wie barocke Musik« (Mozuna)

L'école comporte un bâtiment ovale où ont lieu les cours («le gymnase de l'esprit») et un bâtiment réservé au sport («le gymnase du corps»; en haut, à gauche). Les toits aux larges avant-toits (page de droite) sont des références évidentes à l'architecture japonaise traditionnelle. En bas, à gauche: les classes «légères, rondes et fermées comme la musique baroque» (Mozuna)

KAZUO **SHINOHARA**

The »grey eminence« of contemporary Japanese architecture, Kazuo Shinohara (* 1925) started with Metabolism, then floated between modernist and post-modernist perspective, until he finally settled on a Japanese synthesis of both directions, which he dubbed »Modern Next«. It evolved from the anarchic confusion of forms found in the modern-day megapolis, as Shinohara reveals in his book »Chaos and Machine« (1988), a standard work. From a collage of chunks of rubble, symbols, signposts, overhead wires and leftover forms Shinohara has created a new, graphic architecture: »zero-machines« whose only significance and function consists of reflecting the arbitrariness, confusion and sham of the oppressive metropolis in a constructive manner. Shinohara goes into raptures over the »beauty of progressive urban anarchy«.

Er ist die »graue Eminenz« der zeitgenössischen Architektur in Japan: Kazuo Shinohara (*1925) kam vom Metabolismus. Er schwankte dann zwischen moderner und postmoderner Haltung, bis er schließlich für sich eine japanische Synthese dieser beiden Richtungen fand, die er »Modern Next« nannte. Sie entwickelte sich aus dem anarchischen Formenwirrwarr der heutigen Megapolis, wie Shinohara in seinem Standardwerk »Chaos and Machine« (1988) nachweist. Aus der Collage von Versatzstükken, Zeichen, Beschilderungen, Oberleitungen, Restformen schafft Shinohara eine neue bildhafte Architektur: »Nullpunktmaschinen«, deren einzige Bedeutung und Aufgabe darin bestehen, Beliebigkeit, Zerrissenheit und Schein der geschundenen Metropolen auf eine konstruktive, positive Weise zu spiegeln: Shinohara schwärmt von einer »Schönheit der progressiven Stadtanarchie«.

«Eminence grise» de l'architecture japonaise contemporaine, Kazuo Shinohara (*1925) fut d'abord métaboliste puis hésita entre le modernisme et le post-modernisme pour finalement élaborer une synthèse typiquement japonaise, baptisée par lui «Modern Next», de ces deux mouvements. Comme le décrit Shinohara dans son ouvrage «Chaos and Machine» (1988), celle-ci naît du fourmillement formel anarchique de la mégapole moderne. A partir d'un collage de transpositions, de signes, de descriptions, de formes résiduelles, Shinohara crée une architecture métaphorique, «machines degré zéro», dont la seule signification et la seule mission consistent à reproduire de façon positive l'indifférence, l'écartèlement et l'irréalité des métropoles meurtries. Kazuo Shinohara célèbre la «beauté de l'anarchie progressive».

Chaos is the basic prerequisite of today's city.

Das Chaos ist die Grundvoraussetzung für die Stadt von heute.

Le chaos est la condition d'existence de la ville d'aujourd'hui.

KAZUO SHINOHARA

Uehara House, façade

CENTENNIAL HALL 1987

The Centennial Hall of Tokyo's Institute of Technology adheres to an »aesthetic of chaos«, and in so doing develops a peculiar poetic harmony. The structure, a clubhouse for scientists and guests, is situated right next to a railway, making a play on the contours of a signal-box. Familiar geometric forms like the cylinder and triangle are segmented and fused with one another. Nonetheless, the result is not cacaphony, but rather a dynamic, unified structure – the continuation of Le Corbusier's Ronchamp Chapel.

Die Jahrhunderthalle der Technischen Universität von Tokio gehorcht einer »Ästhetik des Chaos« und entwickelt dabei eine sonderbar poetische Harmonie. Das Bauwerk, ein Clubhaus für Wissenschaftler und Gäste, steht hart an einer Bahnlinie und kokettiert mit der Kontur eines Stellwerks. Bekannte geometrische Formen wie Zylinder oder Dreieck werden gegeneinander verschnitten. Trotzdem entsteht kein Mißklang, sondern ein dynamischer Baukörper, die Fortsetzung der Kapelle von Ronchamp (Le Corbusier).

Le Hall du Siècle de l'université technique de Tokyo obéit à une «esthétique du chaos» et il s'en dégage une étonnante ambiance d'harmonie et de poésie. Le bâtiment, club-house pour les scientifiques et leurs visiteurs, est tout proche d'une ligne de chemin de fer et joue les ressemblances avec un poste d'aiguillage. Des formes géométriques familières, cylindres ou triangles, s'opposent sans fausse note. Au contraire, elles donnent sa dynamique et sa cohésion à cette construction qui se situe dans le prolongement de la chapelle de Le Corbusier à Ronchamp.

A cylindrical monopitch roof is shot through the building like an arrow. Through both form and material, Shinohara makes reference to the adjacent railway environment

Ein zylindrisches Flugdach wird wie ein Pfeil durch das Haus geschossen. Shinohara nimmt mit Form und Material Bezug auf die Sprache der benachbarten Eisenbahnwelt

Un toit cylindrique traverse la maison comme une flèche. Shinohara utilise des formes et des matériaux qui font référence au monde du chemin de fer, tout proche

Gleaming joists from outdoors: within they become a protective »barque« for club-rooms (above; see also floor-plan, right). Climate control installations in the entrance hall (right page) are not hidden, instead becoming design elements in their own right

Der glänzende Balken von außen wird innen zur schützenden Barke für Clubräume (oben, vgl. auch Grundriß rechts). Klima-installationen in der Eingangshalle (rechte Seite) werden nicht versteckt, sondern zu eigenständigen Gestaltungselementen

La poutre brillante à l'extérieur devient, à l'intérieur, nacelle accueillante pour l'espace du club-house (en haut, voir aussi plan, à droite). Dans le hall d'entrée, les installations de climatisation (page de droite) ne sont pas camouflées mais font partie du décor

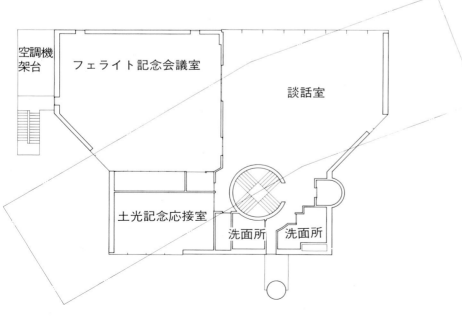

空調機
架台

フェライト記念会議室

談話室

土光記念応接室

洗面所　　洗面所

SHINOHARA HOUSE 1984

Kazuo Shinohara expanded a traditional residence in the hills of Yokohama for himself and his family. He approached the task as though he were a mechanical engineer, the shapes he uses might have been sponsored by NASA or the Navy. The ensemble is an accumulation of what seem to be arbitrarily selected parts. Shinohara has dubbed the result »The Noise of Chance«. It is chance that creates this composition of spaces and views – both inward and out – a surprising living experience.

Kazuo Shinohara hat in den Hügel Yokohamas für sich und seine Familie ein traditionelles Wohnhaus erweitert. Er verhält sich dabei wie ein Maschinenbauer, denn er benutzt Formen, bei denen NASA oder Navy Pate gestanden haben könnten. Das Ensemble ist eine Addition scheinbar willkürlich zusammengesetzter Teile. Shinohara nennt das Ergebnis »Geräusch des Zufalls«. Und der Zufall sorgt hier für eine Komposition aus Räumen, Aus- und Einblicken, für überraschendes Erlebniswohnen.

Shinohara's own home (above and right) is a collage of old and new. Room is still found for the »tatami« in this ascetic spaceship (right page)

Shinoharas eigenes Haus (oben und rechts) ist eine Collage aus alt und neu. Im asketischen Raumschiff bleibt immer noch Platz für die »tatami« (rechte Seite)

La maison personnelle de Shinohara (en haut et à droite) est un collage de vieux et de neuf. Dans ce vaisseau spatial ascétique, les «tatami» ont leur place (page de droite)

Kazuo Shinohara a transformé une maison d'habitation traditionnelle pour lui et sa famille. Tel un constructeur de machine, il l'a fait en utilisant des formes que la NASA et la Navy ne renieraient pas. L'ensemble est une addition de «pièces» que Shinohara décrit commme un «écho du hasard». Et le hasard, donc, se fait complice d'un ensemble d'espaces, de regards sur l'extérieur et sur l'intérieur, bref, d'un habitat surprenant.

SHIN **TAKAMATSU**

Shin Takamatsu (* 1948) wages battle against the »brutal realism of Modernism« and the »Moloch city«, wielding a non-conformist architectural language with a somber, aggressive vocabulary. The Origin Factory in Kyoto has not only been bedecked with metallic clothing – the façades are also »bristling with weapons«. Takamatsu calls it »Dead-Tech«. However, there is more behind such »martial gesticulations« than is visible at first glance. Takamatsu is an aspiring chronicler. His buildings are meant to bear witness to the spirit – and demons – of our time. With the office building Kirin Plaza in Osaka, for example, Takamatsu points out the ambivalence of a society which, on the one hand, uninhibitedly devotes itself to luxury and consumption, while being, on the other, shaken with obscure nightmares. Kirin Plaza consists of four lighthouses of lurid hue with evilly twinkling glass eyes on the façade.

Gegen den »brutalen Realismus der Moderne« und den »Moloch Stadt« tritt Shin Takamatsu (*1948) mit einer eigenen nonkonformistischen Architektursprache aus düster aggressivem Wortschatz an. Der Fabrik Origin in Kioto hat er nicht nur metallene Kleider übergezogen, ihre Fassaden sind auch »waffenbespickt«. Takamatsu nennt es »Dead-Tech«. Hinter solch »martialischen Gebärden« steckt jedoch mehr, als im ersten Augenblick sichtbar wird: Takamatsu will Chronist sein. Seine Gebäude sollen von Geist und Ungeist unserer Zeit zeugen. Mit dem Geschäftshaus Kirin Plaza in Osaka will Takamatsu beispielsweise die Ambivalenz einer Gesellschaft aufzeigen, die sich einerseits hemmungslos dem Luxus und Konsum hingibt und andererseits von geheimnisvollen Alpträumen geschüttelt wird: Kirin Plaza besteht aus vier grellbunten Leuchttürmen mit böse funkelnden Glasaugen an der Fassade.

Au «réalisme brutal de la modernité», face à la «ville Moloch», Shin Takamatsu (*1948) répond par un langage architectural très personnel, au vocabulaire âpre et agressif. L'usine Origin, par exemple, n'est pas seulement revêtue d'une armure métallique, sa façade est «toute lardée d'armes». Takamatsu nomme ce style «dead Tech». Mais, derrière cette allure martiale, il y a autre chose. Takamatsu se veut chroniqueur et ses constructions sont des témoignages de l'esprit et des démons de l'époque. Avec le magasin Kirin Plaza, à Osaka, Takamatsu dénonce l'ambivalence d'une société qui, d'un côté, s'adonne sans retenue au luxe et à la consommation et, d'un autre côté, frissonne de cauchemars terrifiants: Kirin Plaza se compose de quatre phares aux couleurs violentes dont la façade est pourvue d'yeux de verre menaçants.

My buildings are weapons.

Meine Häuser sind Waffen.

Mes maisons sont des armes.

SHIN TAKAMATSU

Cella Building, corner

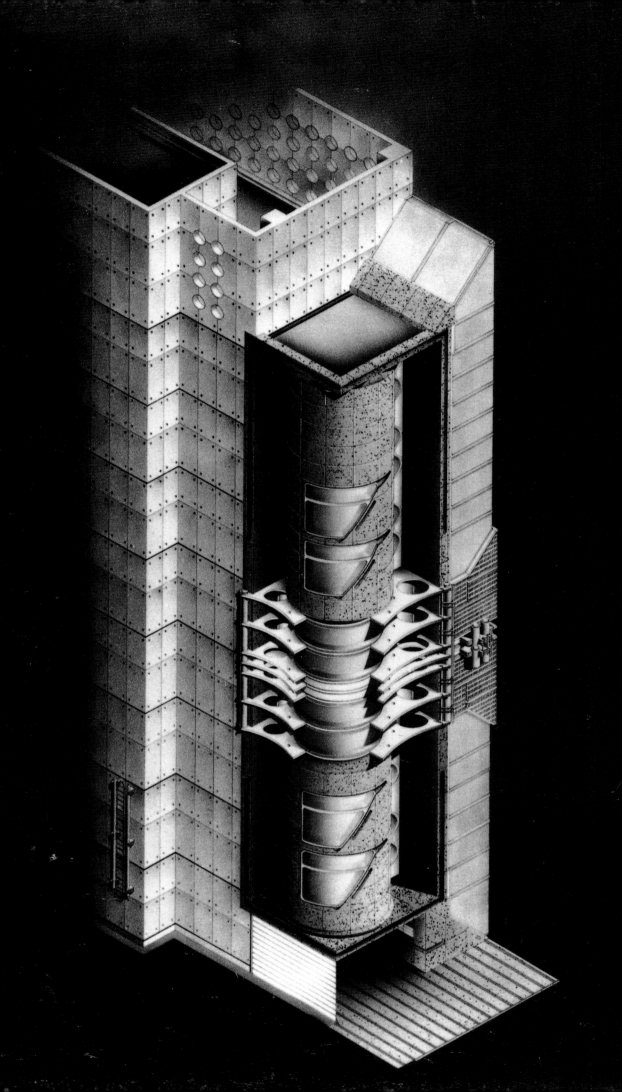

CELLA RETAIL BUILDING 1992

The Cella Building denotes the typical transformation of a Kyoto shopping street. Low wooden buildings give way to six-level office buildings. The Cella Building is lent its particular accent by a rounded bay window. The block's architectural lines will thus be interrupted by a forward-lurching barrel-vault. The Cella Building's façade provides information on Japanese industry's standards of performance: windows and solar deflectors bear the design earmarks of robot-controlled production, already in common use for automobiles and machines.

Das Cella-Haus markiert den typischen Wandel einer Geschäftsstraße in Kioto. Niedrige Holzhäuser machen Platz für sechsgeschossige Geschäftsbauten. Am Cella-Haus setzt Takamatsu unter anderem durch einen Runderker Akzente. Die Baulinie wird durch eine hervorspringende Halbtonne gebrochen. Cellas Fassade gibt Auskunft über den Leistungsstand der japanischen Industrie: Fenster und Sonnenschutz tragen die Gestaltungsmerkmale robotergesteuerter Produktion, wie sie bei Autos und Maschinen üblich sind.

La Maison Cella illustre bien la transformation d'une rue commerçante de Kyoto. Les maisons de bois peu élevées font place à des magasins de six étages. Takamatsu a voulu que le bâtiment porte certains accents, par exemple un encorbellement. L'alignement de maisons sera ainsi brisé par une saillie en demi-tonneau. La façade de la Maison Cella nous en apprend sur le niveau technique de l'industrie japonaise: fenêtres et protections contre le soleil sont fabriquées par des robots, comme pour les pièces de voitures et de machines.

The self-contained block opens out to the street with a rounded bay-window (left page). Japanese cities are sprouting rapidly into the heights (above)

Der geschlossene Quader öffnet sich zur Straße mit Hilfe eines Runderkers (linke Seite). Die japanischen Städte wachsen rasant in die Höhe (oben)

Le parallélépipède fermé s'ouvre sur la rue par un encorbellement (page de gauche). Au Japon, les bâtiments des villes sont de plus en plus hauts (en haut)

SYNTAX BUILDING 1990

Kyoto's Kitayama-dori has rapidly become an exhibition street for Shin Takamatsu's architecture. In addition to his older office buildings »Week«,

»Ining 23« and »Oxy«, the »Syntax« fashion house has arisen on the east end. Each house tells its own story. With »Syntax« it is that of a tremendous ship having dropped anchor. The building's broadly projecting crown is none other than the command bridge of this »consumption steamer«, which appears ready for departure at any moment. Typical Takamatsu: terse metallic details.

Die Kitayama-dori in Kioto ist zur Ausstellungsstraße von Shin Takamatsu geworden: Neben seinen älteren Geschäftshäusern »Week«, »Inning 23« und »Oxy« entstand am östlichen Ende das Modegeschäftshaus »Syntax«. Jedes Haus soll seine Geschichte erzählen. Bei »Syntax« ist es die Story über ein gewaltiges Schiff, das hier vor Anker gegangen ist. Die weit auskragende Hauskrone ist nichts anderes als die Kommandobrücke eines Konsumdampfers, der sich jeden Moment in Bewegung zu setzen scheint. Typisch Takamatsu: schneidige Details aus Metall.

La Kitayama-dori, à Kyoto, est devenue la rue-exposition de Shin Takamatsu: à côté des magasins plus anciens dont il est l'architecte, «Week», «Inning 23» et «Oxy», à l'extrémité est, s'est élevé le magasin de mode «Syntax». Chacun des magasins a une histoire à conter. Pour «Syntax», c'est celle d'un bateau qui aurait jeté l'ancre dans la rue. Le sommet de l'édifice n'est autre que le pont principal d'un paquebot de la consommation qui semble vouloir gagner le large à chaque instant; typique, les détails de métal.

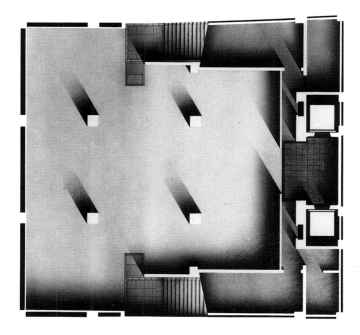

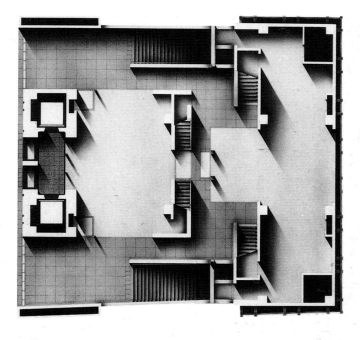

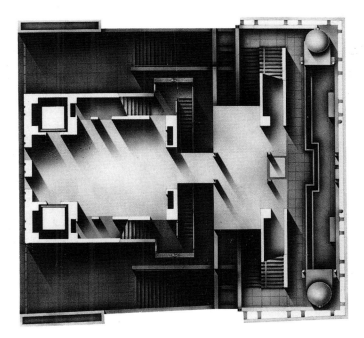

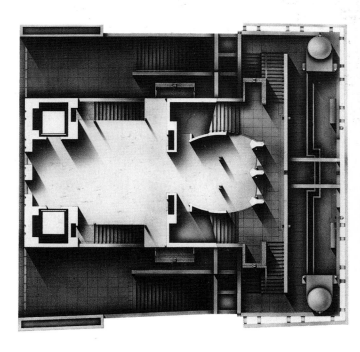

The Syntax Building's ship metaphor becomes very clear in a side elevation (left page). Lower level floor plan (above left); second level (above right); third level (below left); fourth level (below right)

Die Schiffsmetapher wird in der Seitenansicht (linke Seite) überdeutlich. Grundrisse EG (links oben); 1. OG (rechts oben); 2. OG (links unten); 3. OG (rechts unten)

Vu de côté, l'immeuble de «Syntax» apparaît clairement comme un bateau (page de gauche). Plans RC (à gauche en haut); E 1 (à droite, en haut); E 2 (à gauche, en bas); E 3 (à droite, en bas)

One can set foot on the »consumption steamer«: the sweeping outdoor stairways function as »animators« for the Syntax Building's luxury boutiques. Along their steps the entire selection can be viewed through curved windows

Der Konsumdampfer ist begehbar: Die geschwungenen Außentreppen funktionieren als »Animateur« der Edelboutiquen im Syntax-Haus: Hinter gebogenen Gläsern ist das gesamte Angebot zu besichtigen

Le paquebot de la consommation est ouvert au public: des escaliers extérieurs tout en courbe incitent à pénétrer dans les boutiques luxueuses de la Maison «Syntax»: derrière des vitres bombées, on peut voir les étalages

IMANISHI BUILDING 1991

There is no mistaking the fact that Shin Takamatsu has sacrificed his usual martial gestures to a gentler design standard in his more recent buildings. Even so, the »voracious grimace of an egghead« is a kind of symbolic declaration of war on the City of Consumption. The number of storeys grows as the extremely narrow parcels of land in Kyoto and Tokyo make for an architecture of the vertical, which Takamatsu further emphasizes through the use of recessed sash bars.

Es ist unverkennbar, daß Shin Takamatsu in seinen jüngeren Gebäuden die gewohnte martialische Geste einem sanfteren Formenkanon opfert. Doch immer noch ist die »gefräßige Grimasse eines Eggheads« eine Art symbolische Kriegserklärung an die Konsum-City. Die sehr schmalen Grundstücksparzellen in Kioto und Tokio sorgen bei steigender Geschoßzahl für eine Architektur der Vertikalen. Takamatsu betont sie durch enggelegte Fenstersprossung.

Les constructions récentes de Shin Takamatsu renoncent aux symboles guerriers au profit d'une esthétique plus douce. Mais la «grimace gourmande d'une tête d'œuf» que fait cet immeuble est encore une déclaration de guerre symbolique à la ville de consommation. Les terrains très exigus de Kyoto ou Tokyo expliquent le choix d'une architecture verticale. Takamatsu souligne cette verticalité par une éclosion de fenêtres très proches les unes des autres.

The narrow gap-filler looks like a cathedral of consumption (left page and below left). This impression is confirmed in the salesrooms (above left)

Der schlanke Lückenfüller wirkt wie eine Kathedrale des Konsums (linke Seite und unten links). Dieser Eindruck wird in den Verkaufsräumen bestätigt (oben links)

L'immeuble qui vient boucher l'étroit espace, semble une cathédrale de la consommation (page de gauche et en bas, à gauche). La même impression se dégage des espaces de vente intérieurs (en haut, à gauche)

RIKEN **YAMAMOTO**

Just as in Europe or the USA, residential construction is not the Japanese avant-garde's pre-eminent field of activity. Riken Yamamoto (*1945) is considered a lonely voice in the urban wilderness. His residences are small and clearly organized, unfolding in the only direction left in view of the scarce and overpriced land: upward. Yamamoto's trademarks are his eccentric roof constructions. They remind one of a ship's tarpaulin or an oversized sun-umbrella. He exaggerates dimensions and creates particularly elaborate designs because he wants to make a point. Yamamoto takes his bearings from the basic features of historical Japanese residences. His roof structures are lightweight, the walls transparent, and transitions between indoors and out fluid: when the Japanese garden falls victim to real-estate speculation, it is relocated on the roof.

Wie in Europa oder den USA ist der Wohnungsbau nicht das vorrangige Betätigungsfeld der japanischen Avantgarde. Riken Yamamoto (*1945) gilt als der einsame Rufer in der (Stadt-)Wüste. Seine Wohnhäuser sind klein und klar gegliedert und entwickeln sich in die einzige Richtung, die der knappe und überteuerte Grund zuläßt: nach oben. Yamamotos Gütezeichen sind ausgefallene Dachkonstruktionen. Sie erinnern an die Persenning eines Schiffes oder an übergroße Sonnenschirme. Er übertreibt bei der Dimensionierung und gestaltet besonders aufwendig, weil er Zeichen setzen möchte. Yamamoto orientiert sich an den Eigenschaften des historischen japanischen Wohnhauses: Seine Dachaufbauten sind leicht, die Wände transparent, die Übergänge zwischen Innen und Außen fließend. Wenn der japanische Garten Opfer der Bodenspekulation wird, verlegt man ihn einfach auf das Dach.

Comme c'est le cas en Europe ou aux Etats-Unis, la construction de maisons particulières n'est pas la spécialité de l'avant-garde japonaise. Riken Yamamoto (*1945) fait figure d'exception. Ses maisons sont petites, structurées et se développent dans la seule direction laissée ouverte par l'exiguïté et les prix du terrain: en hauteur. La marque de Yamamoto, c'est une grande originalité en matière de toits. On pense aux prélarts d'un bateau ou à des parasols. S'ils sont de dimensions aussi grandes et d'une conception aussi élaborée c'est que Yamamoto les considère comme les signes de ponctuation de la phrase architecturale. L'architecte s'inspire des données historiques. Les structures de ses toits sont légères, les murs sont transparents, les espaces intérieurs et extérieurs coulent les uns dans les autres. Lorsque le jardin japonais est malade de la spéculation immobilière, on le transporte sur le toit.

The roof is the most important point in the building, it brings people together.

Das Dach ist der wichtigste Punkt im Haus, es bringt die Menschen zusammen.

Le toit est le point primordial de la maison, c'est lui qui rassemble les gens.

RIKEN YAMAMOTO

Rotunda Building, façade

HAMLET BUILDING 1988

The traditional small wooden dwellings still exist in the Tokyo district of Shibuya-ku, though they are increasingly being replaced by commercial office blocks. Thus, in this part of Tokyo new residential housing is the exception. Three generations of one family live in the light, airy structure of Hamlet. The individual rooms, which are independent cottages in themselves, are suspended in a filigreed steel structure. Additional spaces are created for the children below semicircular canvas roofs. In its form Hamlet is a repudiation of the miserable residential boxes that were common to post-war Japan.

Noch existieren in Tokio, im Stadtteil Shibuya-ku, die üblichen kleinen Wohnhäuser aus Holz. Sie werden zunehmend durch kommerzielle Büroblocks ersetzt. Ein neues Wohnhaus ist an dieser Stelle Tokios deswegen untypisch. In der leichten und luftigen Konstruktion von »Hamlet« leben drei Generationen einer Familie. Die einzelnen Zimmer wurden als selbständige Häuschen in die filigrane Stahlkonstruktion gehängt. Unter halbkreisförmigen Segeltuchdächern entstand zusätzlicher Raum für die Kinder. Formal ist »Hamlet« eine Absage an die gemeine Hausschachtel, wie sie im Nachkriegsjapan üblich war.

Il existe encore à Tokyo, dans le quartier de Shibuya-ku, les traditionnelles petites maisons de bois japonaises. De plus en plus, elle sont remplacées par des immeubles de bureaux. C'est pourquoi une nouvelle maison d'habitation dans cette partie de la ville est chose étonnante. Dans ce bâtiment, baptisé «Hamlet», léger et aéré, vivent trois générations d'une même famille. Chaque pièce est une petite maison en soi, suspendue dans l'ossature filiforme en acier. Des toits hémisphériques en toile de bâche abritent un espace supplémentaire pour les enfants. «Hamlet» est un manifeste contre la maison-clapier telle qu'elle était construite dans le Japon de l'après-guerre.

A dynamically arched roof (right page and outer left) gives the house the character of »flying buildings«. Drawing: view of roof

Das dynamisch gebogene Dach (links außen und rechte Seite) verleiht dem Wohnhaus den Charakter »fliegender Bauten«. Zeichnung: Dachaufsicht

La ligne dynamique du toit (à l'extrême gauche et page de droite) «donne des ailes» à cette maison. Dessin: vue du toit

RYUKOEN-TOSHI DEVELOPMENT 1992

The success of his smaller residential structures has inspired Yamamoto to apply his principles in larger housing developments as well. Even now, his buildings give the impression of being light and easily disassembled. The architect dissects such complexes using the human organism as his model, with self-sufficient cells for separate, individually designed living units. The key element ordering and unifying the whole is a covered gallery with public staircases.

Die Erfolge seiner kleinen Wohnhäuser haben Yamamoto beflügelt, seine Prinzipien auch in größeren Wohnanlagen anzuwenden. Und auch dann wirken seine Bauten noch leicht und demontabel. Yamamoto zerlegt solche Wohnanlagen nach dem Vorbild eines menschlichen Organismus in autarke Zellen für die einzelnen, individuell gestalteten Wohnungen. Ordnungs- und Verbindungselement bildet eine gedeckte Galerie mit öffentlichen Treppenhäusern.

Le succès de ses petites maisons particulières a encouragé Yamamoto à appliquer ses principes à de plus grands ensembles d'habitation. Mais, là encore, ses constructions gardent leur légèreté. Elles sont conçues sur le schéma de l'organisme humain, en cellules indépendantes donnant lieu à des espaces de vie individuels. L'élément unificateur est une galerie couverte avec ses escaliers extérieurs.

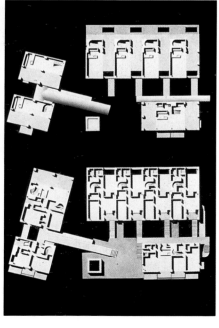

The individual town houses are grouped
around a covered passage (left and right
pages). Left: floor plan overview

Die einzelnen Stadthäuser gruppieren sich
um eine überdachte Passage (links außen
und rechte Seite): Links: Grundrißüberblick

Les différentes maisons sont regroupées
autour d'un passage couvert (à gauche et
page de droite). A gauche: plan général

Transparency has a tradition in Japan.
Yamamoto achieves it with glass and perforated metal plates, even using them for
steps and landings

Transparenz hat in Japan Tradition. Yamamoto erzeugt sie dank Glas und Lochblech
sogar an Treppenstufen und Geländern

La transparence des cloisons est un élément
japonais traditionnel. Yamamoto les a vou-
lues en verre ou en tôle perforée, même
pour les marches d'escalier et les rampes

BIOGRAPHIES

TADAO ANDO

Born 1941 in Osaka. Autodidact, private practice since 1969 in Osaka
Important buildings: Townhouses (Azuma House), Osaka (1976); Rokko Apartments, Kobe (1983); Chapel on Mount Rokko, Kobe (1986); Time's Buildings I & II, Kyoto (1984, 1991); Church on the Water, Hokkaido (1988); Church of Lights, Osaka (1989); RAIKA Headquarters, Osaka (1989); Water Temple, Awaji Hyogo (1991); Japanese Pavilion, Sevilla Expo (1992)
Award: Carlsberg Prize for Architecture, Denmark 1992
Address: Tadao Ando Architect & Associates, 5-23 Toyosaki 2-Chome Kita-ku, Osaka 531, Japan.
Fax 06-3746-240

Geboren 1941 in Osaka. Autodidakt, eigenes Büro seit 1969 in Osaka.
Wichtige Bauten: Reihenhäuser (Azuma-Haus), Osaka (1976); Rokko Apartments, Kobe (1983); Kapelle am Mount Rokko, Kobe (1986); Time's Buildings I und II, Kioto (1984, 1991); Kirche auf dem Wasser, Hokkaido (1988); Kirche des Lichts, Osaka (1989); RAIKA-Hauptquartier, Osaka (1989); Wassertempel, Awaji Hyogo (1991); Japanischer Pavillon, Expo Sevilla (1992)
Auszeichnung: Carlsberg-Architekturpreis, Dänemark 1992

Anschrift: Tadao Ando Architect & Associates., 5–23 Toyosaki 2-Chome Kita-ku, Osaka 531, Japan.
Fax 06-3746-240

Né en 1941 à Osaka. Autodidacte, a ses propres bureaux depuis 1969 à Osaka
Principales réalisations: petites maisons d'habitation (Maison Azuma), Osaka (1976); Rokko Apartments, Kobe (1983); Chapelle du Mont Rokko, Kobe (1986); Time's Building I et II, Kyoto (1984, 1991); Eglise sur l'eau, Hokkaido (1988); Eglise de la lumière, Osaka (1989); RAIKA-Headquarter, Osaka (1989); Temple de l'eau, Awaji Hyogo (1991); Pavillon japonais de l'exposition de Séville (1992)
Récompense: prix d'architecture Carlsberg, Danemark 1992
Adresse: Tadao Ando Architect & Associates, 5-23 Toyosaki 2-Chome Kita-ku, Osaka 531, Japan.
Fax 06-3746-240

HIROMI FUJII

Born 1935 in Tokyo. Degree from the University of Waseda in 1958.
Periods of study in Milan and London, private practice since 1968. Professor at the Shibaura Institute of Technology
Important buildings: Myata Building (1980); Ushimado Centre for the Arts (1985); Gymnasium II for the Shibaura Institute of Technology (1986); Mizoe House I, Iizuku (1988); Installation at the Europalia Exhibition, Brussels (1989)
Address: Fujii Studio, 9-14 Shibaura, 3 chome Minato-ku, Tokyo, Japan.
Fax 03-5476-3168

Geboren 1935 in Tokio. Diplom an der Universität Waseda 1958. Studienaufenthalte in Mailand und London, eigenes Büro seit 1968. Professor am Shibaura Institute of Technology
Wichtige Bauten: Myata-Haus (1980); Ushimado-Kunstzentrum (1985); Zweite Turnhalle des Shibaura Institute of Technology (1986); Mizoe-Haus 1, Iizuku (1988); Installation auf der Europalia-Messe, Brüssel (1989)
Anschrift: Fujii Studio, 9-14 Shibaura, 3 chome Minato-ku, Tokio, Japan.
Fax 03-5476-3168

Né en 1935 à Tokyo. Diplôme à l'université de Waseda 1958. Séjours d'étude à Milan et Londres. A son propre bureau depuis 1968. Professeur à l'Institut technologique de Shibaura
Principales réalisations: Maison Myata (1980); Centre artistique Ushimado (1985); deuxième gymnase de l'Institut technologique de Shibaura (1986); Maison Mizoe 1, Iizuka (1988); stand de Europalia, Bruxelles (1989)
Adresse: Fujii Studio, 9-14 Shibaura, 3 chome Minato-ku, Tokyo, Japan. Fax 03-5476-3168

HIROSHI HARA

Born 1936 in Nagano. Diploma in Tokyo 1959, doctorate 1964.
Founded his first studio in 1970, Professor in Tokyo since 1970
Important buildings: Awazu House, Kawasaki (1972); Hara House, Machida (1974); Nakatsuku House, Ito (1982); Yamato International, Tokyo (1987); Sotetsu Cultural Centre, Yokohama (1990); JR Station Project, Kyoto (1993); Umeda City, Osaka (1993)
Address: Hiroshi Hara and StudioΦ, Daikanyama Edge Building 5f, 28-10 Sarugaku-cho, Shibuyaku, Tokyo 150, Japan. Fax 03-3464-8612

Geboren 1936 in Nagano. Diplom in Tokio 1959, Promotion 1964. Gründung des ersten Ateliers 1970, seit 1970 Professor in Tokio
Wichtige Bauten: Haus Awazu, Kawasaki (1972); Haus Hara, Machida (1974); Haus Nakatsuku, Ito (1982); Yamato International, Tokio (1987); Sotetsu-Kulturzentrum, Yokohama (1990); Projekt JR Station, Kioto (1993); Umeda City, Osaka (1993)
Anschrift: Hiroshi Hara und Atelier Φ, Daikanyama Edge Building 5F, 28-10 Sarugaku-cho, Shibuyaku, Tokio 150, Japan. Fax 03-3464-8612

Né en 1936 à Nagano. Diplôme à Tokyo 1959, doctorat en 1964. Fondation du premier atelier en 1970. Depuis 1970, professeur à Tokyo
Principales réalisations: Maison Awazu, Kawasaki (1972); Maison Hara, Machida (1974); Maison Nakatsuku, Ito (1982); Yamato International, Tokyo (1987); Centre culturel de Sotetsu, Yokohama (1990); Projet JR Station, Kyoto (1993); Umeda City, Osaka (1993)
Adresse: Hiroshi Hara et Atelier Φ, Daikanyama Edge Building 5F, 28-10 Sarugaku-cho, Shibuyaku, Tokyo 150, Japan. Fax 03-3464-8612

ITSUKO HASEGAWA

Born 1941 in the Shizuoka Prefecture. Degree from the Kanto Gakuin University in Yokohama 1964. Assistant of Kazuo Shinohara. Private practice since 1979
Important buildings: Tokumaru Children's Hospital (1979); Kuwahara House, Matsuyama (1980); AONO Building, Matsuyama (1982); Sugai Hospital in Matsuyama (1986); Shonandai Cultural Centre, Fujisawa (1989); Cona Village, Amagasaki (1990); S.T.M. House, Tokyo (1991)
Address: Itsuko Hasegawa Studio, 1-9-7 Yushima Bunkyo-ku, Tokyo, Japan. Fax 03-3818-2244

Geboren 1941 in der Präfektur Shizuoka. Diplom 1964 an der Universität Kanto Gakuin in Yokohoma. Assistentin bei Shinohara; 1979 Atelier
Wichtige Bauten: Kinderkrankenhaus Tokumaru (1979); Haus Kuwahara, Matsuyama (1980); AONO-Haus, Matsuyama (1982); Krankenhaus Sugai in Matsuyama (1986); Shonandai-Kulturzentrum, Fujisawa (1989); Cona Village, Amagasaki (1990); S.T.M.-Haus, Tokio (1991)
Anschrift: Itsuko Hasegawa Atelier, 1-9-7 Yushima Bunkyo-ku, Tokio, Japan. Fax 03-3818-2244

Née en 1941 dans la préfecture de Shizuoka. Diplôme en 1964 à l'université de Kanto Gakuin à Yokohama. Assistante de Kazuo Shinohara. A son propre atelier depuis 1979

Principales réalisations: Hôpital pour enfants de Tokumaru (1979); Maison Kuwahara, Matsuyama (1980); Maison AONO, Matsuyama (1982); Hôpital Sugai, Matsuyama (1986); Centre culturel Shonandai, Fujisawa (1989); Cona Village, Amagasaki (1990); Maison S.T.M, Tokyo (1991)

Adresse: Itsuko Hasegawa Atelier, 1-9-7 Yushima Bunkyo-ku, Tokyo, Japan. Fax 03-3818-2244

KATSUHIRO ISHII

Born 1944 in Tokyo. Studied until 1975 under Arata Isozaki, Charles Moore (USA) and James Stirling (London) among others; private practice since 1976

Important buildings: House with 54 Windows, Hiratsuka (1975); Gable Building, Tokyo (1980); personal residence (1983); Sukiya-yu, Okayama (1989); Theatre and Exhibition Hall Bunraku, Kumamoto Prefecture (1992)

Address: Katsuhiro Ishii Architect & Associates, Akasaka Studio, 4-14-27 Akasaka, Minato-ku, Tokyo, Japan. Fax 03-505-0766

Geboren 1944 in Tokio; Studium bis 1975 u. a. bei Arata Isozaki, Charles Moore (USA) und James Stirling (London); eigenes Büro seit 1976

Wichtige Bauten: Haus mit 54 Fenstern, Hiratsuka (1975); Giebelhaus, Tokio (1980); eigenes Haus (1983); Sukiya-yu, Okayama (1989); Theater und Ausstellungshalle Bunraku, Präfektur Kumamoto (1992)

Anschrift: Katsuhiro Ishii Architect & Associates, Akasaka Studio, 4-14-27 Akasaka, Minato-ku, Tokio, Japan. Fax 03-505-0766

Né en 1944 à Tokyo. Etudes jusqu'en 1975 auprès de Arata Isozaki, Charles Moore (Etats-Unis) et James Stirling (Londres). A son propre bureau depuis 1976

Principales réalisations: Maison aux 54 fenêtres, Hiratsuka (1975); Maison aux frontons, Tokyo (1980); maison personnelle (1983); Sukiya-yu, Okayama (1989); Théâtre et hall d'exposition à Bunraku, dans la préfecture de Kumamoto (1992)

Adresse: Katsuhiro Ishii Architect & Associates, Akasaka Studio, 4-14-27 Akasaka, Minato-ku, Tokyo, Japan. Fax 03-505-0766

ARATA ISOZAKI

Born 1931 in Oita. Degree from the University of Tokyo in 1954; employee of Kenzo Tange 1954-1963, independent since 1963

Important buildings: Medical Centre, Oita (1960); Festival Plaza, Expo Osaka (1970); Gunma Museum of Visual Arts, Takasaki City (1974); Fujimi Golf Club, Oita (1974); Kitakyushu Central Library (1974); Western Japanese Exhibition Centre, Kitakyushu (1977); Tsukuba Centre (1983); Museum of Contemporary Art, Los Angeles (1986); Musashi-kyuryo Golf Club, Saitama (1987); Olympic Sports Hall, Barcelona (1990); Congress Centre, Kitakyushu (1990); Art Tower, Mito (1990); Disney Building, Orlando (1990); Brooklyn Museum (under construction)

Award: Chicago Prize for Architecture 1990

Address: Arata Isozaki & Associates, 9-6-17 Akasaka, Minato-ku, Tokyo 107, Japan. Fax 03-3475-5265

Geboren 1931 in Oita; Diplom an der Universität Tokio 1954; 1954-1963 Mitarbeiter bei Kenzo Tange; seit 1963 selbständig

Wichtige Bauten: Medizinisches Zentrum, Oita (1960); Festival Plaza, Expo Osaka (1970); Gunma-Museum für bildende Kunst, Takasaki City (1974); Golfclub Fujimi, Oita

(1974); Zentralbibliothek Kitakyushu (1974); Westjapanisches Ausstellungszentrum, Kitakyushu (1977); Tsukuba Center (1983); Museum of Contemporary Art, Los Angeles (1986); Golfklub Musashi-kyuryo, Saitama (1987); Olympiasporthalle, Barcelona (1990); Kongreßzentrum, Kitakyushu (1990); Kunstturm, Mito (1990); Disney Building, Orlando (1990); Brooklyn Museum (im Bau)
Auszeichnung: Chicago-Architekturpreis 1990
Anschrift: Arata Isozaki & Associates, 9-6-17 Akasaka, Minato-ku, Tokio 107, Japan. Fax 03-3475-5265

Né en 1931 à Oita. Diplôme à l'université de Tokyo en 1954; de 1954 à 1963 travaille chez Kenzo Tange; installé à son compte depuis 1963
Principales réalisations: Centre médical, Oita (1960); Festival Plaza, Expo Osaka (1970); Musée Gunma pour les arts plastiques, Takasaki City (1974); Golfclub de Fujimi, Oita (1974); Bibliothèque centrale de Kitakyushu (1974); Centre d'exposition du Japon de l'ouest, Kitakyushu (1977); Tsukuba Center (1983); Museum of Contemporary Art, Los Angeles (1986); Golfclub de Musashi-kyuryo, Saitama (1987); Halle de sports olympique, Barcelone (1990): Centre des congrès, Kitakyushu (1990); Tour de l'Art, Mito (1990);

Disney Building, Orlando, Floride (1990); Brooklyn Museum (en construction)
Récompense: prix d'architecture de la ville de Chicago 1990
Adresse: Arata Isozaki & Associates, 9-6-17 Akasaka, Minato-ku, Tokyo 107, Japan. Fax 03-3475-5265

TOYO ITO

Born 1941 in Seoul, Korea. Degree in 1965 from the University of Tokyo. Private practice since 1971
Important buildings: House of Aluminium (1971); U-House, Nakano (1976); Hotel D, Nagano (1977); PMT Building, Nagoya (1978); Silver Hut (1984); Tower of Winds, Yokohama (1986); House in Magomezawa (1986); Nomad Club, Tokyo (1986); Egg of Winds (1989); Guest House for Sapporo Brewery, Eniwa (1989); Museum, Yatsuhiro (1991)
Address: Toyo Ito & Associates Architects, 10-12 Minamiaoyama 5-Chome, Minato-ku, Tokyo 107, Japan. Fax 03-409-5969

Geboren 1941 in Seoul/Korea. Diplom 1965 an der Universität Tokio. Eigenes Büro seit 1971
Wichtige Bauten: Haus aus Aluminium (1971); U-Haus, Nakano

(1976); Hotel D, Nagano (1977); PMT-Haus, Nagoya (1978); Silver Hut (1984); Turm der Winde, Yokohama (1986); Haus in Magomezawa (1986); Nomad Club, Tokio (1986); Egg of Winds (1989); Gästehaus der Sapporo-Brauerei, Eniwa (1989); Museum, Yatsuhiro (1991)
Anschrift: Toyo Ito & Associates Architects, 10-12 Minamiaoyama 5-Chome, Minato-ku, Tokio 107, Japan. Fax 03-409-5969

Né en 1941 à Séoul, Corée. Diplôme en 1965 à l'université de Tokyo. A son propre bureau depuis 1971
Principales réalisations: Maison en aluminium (1971); Maison-U, Nakano (1976); Hôtel D, Nagano (1977); Maison PMT, Nagoya (1978); Silver Hut (1984); Tour des vents, Yokohama (1986); Maison à Magomezawa (1986); Nomad Club, Tokyo (1986); Egg of Winds (1989); Maison des hôtes de la brasserie Sapporo, Eniwa (1989); Musée, Yatsuhiro (1991)
Adresse: Toyo Ito & Associates Architects, 10-12 Minamiaoyama 5-Chome, Minato-ku, Tokyo 107, Japan. Fax 03-409-5969

KISHO KUROKAWA

Born 1934 in Nagoya. Diploma in Tokyo 1960. Employee of Kenzo Tange. Private practice since 1961. Active member of the Metabolists.
Important buildings: Capsule Pavilion, Expo Osaka (1970); Sony Highrise, Osaka (1976); Saitama Prefecture Museum of Modern Art, Urawa (1982); National Bunraku Theatre, Osaka (1983); Municipal Museum of Art, Nagoya (1987); Deutsch-japanisches Zentrum, Berlin (1988); Museum of Contemporary Art, Hiroshima (1988); Polar Expedition Monument, Akita (1990); Melbourne Central (1991)
Award: Prize of the Japanese Architectural Institute 1990
Address: Kisho Kurokawa, Architect & Associates; Aoyama Bldg. 11f, 1-2-3 Kita-Aoyama, Minato-ku, Tokyo, Japan. Fax 03-3404-6222

Geboren 1934 in Nagoya. 1960 Diplom in Tokio. Mitarbeit bei Kenzo Tange. Eigenes Büro seit 1961. Aktives Mitglied der Metabolisten
Wichtige Bauten: Kapsel-Pavillon Expo, Osaka (1970); Sony-Hochhaus, Osaka (1976); Saitama-Präfektur-Museum der modernen Kunst, Urawa (1982); National Bunraku Theater, Osaka (1983); Städtisches Kunstmuseum, Nagoya (1987);

Deutsch-japanisches Zentrum, Berlin (1988); Museum für zeitgenössische Kunst, Hiroshima (1988); Polarexpeditions-Denkmal in Akita (1990); Melbourne Central (1991)
Auszeichnung: Preis des japanischen Architekturinstituts 1990
Anschrift: Kisho Kurokawa, Architect & Associates; Aoyama Bldg. 11f, 1-2-3 Kita-Aoyama, Minato-ku, Tokio, Japan. Fax 03-3404-6222

Né en 1934 à Nagoya. Diplôme à Tokyo en 1960. Travaille chez Kenzo Tange. A son propre bureau depuis 1961. Membre actif des métabolistes
Principales réalisations: Pavillon capsule, Expo Osaka (1970); Tour Sony, Osaka (1976); Musée d'art moderne de la préfecture de Saitama, Urawa (1982); National Bunraku Theater, Osaka (1983); Musée d'art de la ville de Nagoya (1987); Deutsch-japanisches Zentrum, Berlin (1988); Musée d'art contemporain, Hiroshima (1988); Monument aux expéditions polaires, Akita (1990); Melbourne Central (1991)
Récompense: prix de l'Institut d'architecture japonais, 1990
Adresse: Kisho Kurokawa, Architect & Associates, Aoyama Bldg. 11f, 1-2-3 Kita-Aoyama, Minato-ku, Tokyo, Japan. Fax 03-3404-6222

FUMIHIKO MAKI

Born 1928 in Tokyo. Diploma 1954 in Tokyo; training at Skidmore, Owings & Merrill (Chicago) and José Lluis Sert (Barcelona). Private practice since 1965
Important buildings: Toyota Memorial Hall, Nagoya (1960); Rowhouses on a Slope, Tokyo (1969-1979); Spiral Building, Tokyo (1985); National Museum of Art, Kyoto (1986); Fujisawa Sports Hall and Sports Hall with indoor swimming pool, Tokyo (1984-1990); TEPIA Building, Tokyo (1989)
Address: Maki and Associates, 3-6-2 Nihonbashi, Chuoh-ku, Tokyo 103, Japan. Fax 03-3273-4871

Geboren 1928 in Tokio. Diplom 1954 in Tokio, Lehrjahre bei Skidmore, Owings & Merrill (Chicago) und José Lluis Sert (Barcelona). Eigenes Büro seit 1965
Wichtige Bauten: Toyota Memorial Hall, Nagoya (1960); Reihenhäuser am Hang, Tokio (1969-1979); Spiral-Haus, Tokio (1985); Nationales Kunstmuseum, Kioto (1986); Sporthalle Fujisawa und Sporthalle mit Schwimmhalle, Tokio (1984-1990); TEPIA-Haus, Tokio (1989)
Anschrift: Maki and Associates, 3-6-2 Nihonbashi, Chuoh-ku, Tokio 103, Japan. Fax 03-3273-4871

Né en 1928 à Tokyo. Diplôme en 1954 à Tokyo. Etudie auprès de Skidmore, Owings & Merrill (Chicago) et José Lluis Sert (Barcelone). A son propre bureau depuis 1965
Principales réalisations: Toyota Memorial Hall, Nagoya (1960); Maisons sur la colline, Tokyo (1969-1979); Maison-Spirale, Tokyo (1985); Musée d'art national, Kyoto (1986); Palais des sports Fujisawa et Palais des sports et piscine, Tokyo (1984-1990); Maison TEPIA, Tokyo (1989)
Adresse: Maki & Associates, 3-6-2 Nihonbashi, Chuoh-ku, Tokyo 103, Japan. Fax 03-3273-4871

KIKO MOZUNA

Born 1941 in Kushiro City. Degree in 1965 from the University of Kobe. Private practice since 1969
Important buildings: Anti-Box-for-Living, Kushiro (1972); Zen Temple, Tokyo (1979); two museums in Kushiro (1984); Unoki Elementary School, Wakami (1988); Museum, Nagano (1989); Monzen Family Inn, Ishikawa (1991); Museum of Glass Art, Noto island (1991)
Address: Kiko Mozuna Architects & Associates, 6-5-29 Ookura Setagaya-ku, Tokyo 157, Japan. Fax 03-374-92719

Geboren 1941 in Kushiro City. Diplom 1965 an der Universität von Kobe. Eigenes Büro seit 1969
Wichtige Bauten: Anti-Wohnkiste, Kushiro (1972); Zen-Tempel, Tokio (1979); Zwei Museen in Kushiro (1984); Unoki-Grundschule, Wakami (1988); Museum, Nagano (1989); Monzen-Hotel, Ishikawa (1991); Glaskunstmuseum, Noto Island (1991)
Anschrift: Kiko Mozuna Architects & Associates, 6-5-29 Ookura Setagaya-ku, Tokio 157, Japan. Fax 03-374-92719

Né en 1941 à Kushiro City. Diplôme en 1965 à l'université de Kobe. A son propre bureau depuis 1969
Principales réalisations: Anti-clapier, Kushiro (1972); Temple Zen, Tokyo (1979); deux musées à Kushiro (1984); Ecole primaire de Unoki, Wakami (1988); Musée, Nagano (1989); Hôtel Monzen, Ishikawa (1991); Musée du verre, île de Noto (1991)
Adresse: Kiko Mozuna Architects & Associates, 6-5-29 Ookura Setagaya-ku, Tokyo 157, Japan. Fax 03-374-92719

KAZUO SHINOHARA

Born 1925 in Shizuoka Prefecture. Degree from the Tokyo Technical University 1953. Since 1953 instructor there, full professor since 1970
Important buildings: Umbrella House, Tokyo (1961); House in White, Tokyo (1966); Cubical Forest Lodge, Kawasaki (1971); House in Uehara (1976); Shinohara House, Yokohama (1984); Centennial Hall for the Tokyo Institute of Technology (1987); Police Headquarters, Kumamoto (1990)
Address: Shinohara Studio, 1622 Futoocho, Kohoku-ku, Yokohama 222, Japan. Fax 045-544-6099

Geboren 1925 in der Präfektur Shizuoka. Diplom 1953 an der Technischen Universität Tokio. Seit 1953 Lehrer an dieser Hochschule, seit 1970 ordentlicher Professor
Wichtige Bauten: Regenschirmhaus, Tokio (1961); Haus in Weiß, Tokio (1966); kubisches Waldhaus, Kawasaki (1971); Haus in Uehara (1976); Haus Shinohara, Yokohama (1984); Jahrhunderthalle der Technischen Universität Tokio (1987); Polizeihauptquartier, Kumamoto (1990)
Anschrift: Shinohara Atelier, 1622 Futoocho, Kohoku-ku, Yokohama 222, Japan. Fax 045-544-6099

Né en 1925 dans la préfecture de Shizuoka. Diplôme en 1953 à l'université technique de Tokyo. Puis assistant à cet établissement dont il devient professeur en 1970
Principales réalisations: Maison-parapluie, Tokyo (1961); Maison en blanc, Tokyo (1966); Maison-cube forestière, Kawasaki (1971); Maison à Uehara (1976); Maison Shinohara, Yokohama (1984); Hall du siècle de l'université technique de Tokyo (1987); Quartier général de la police, Kumamoto (1990)
Adresse: Shinohara Atelier, 1622 Futoocho, Kohoku-ku, Yokohama 222, Japan. Fax 045-544-6099

SHIN TAKAMATSU

Born 1948 in Shimane. Degree from the University of Kyoto 1971. Doctorate 1980. Private practice since 1980. Instructor at the Art Academy of Osaka and the Kyoto Technical College
Important buildings: Koakine Building, Hyogo (1977); Origin I, Kyoto (1981); Saifukuji Temple, Kani (1982); Ark Dental Clinic, Kyoto (1983); Week Office Building, Kyoto (1986); Origin III, Kyoto (1986); Kirin Plaza, Osaka (1986); Ining 23, Kyoto (1987); Syntax Building, Kyoto (1990); Solaris Building, Amagasaki (1988); Oxy (office building), Kyoto (1989); Imanishi Motoakasaka (office building), Tokyo (1991); Cella Retail Building, Kyoto (1992)
Award: Prize of the Biennale in Venice 1985
Address: Takamatsu & Lahyani, 36-4 Jyobodaiin-cho, Takeda Fushimi-ku, Kyoto, Japan 612. Fax 075-621-6079

Geboren 1948 in Shimane, Diplom an der Kioto-Universität 1971. Promotion 1980. Eigenes Büro seit 1980. Lehrte an der Kunstakademie in Osaka und der Technischen Hochschule Kioto
Wichtige Bauten: Koakine-Haus, Hyogo (1977); Origin I, Kioto (1981); Saifukuji-Tempel, Kani (1982); Zahnklinik Ark, Kioto (1983); Geschäftshaus Week, Kioto (1986); Origin III, Kioto (1986); Kirin Plaza, Osaka (1986); Geschäftshaus Ining 23, Kioto (1987); Syntax-Haus, Kioto (1990); Solaris-Haus, Amagasaki (1988); Geschäftshaus Oxy, Kioto (1989); Geschäftshaus Imanishi Motoakasaka, Tokio (1991); Geschäftshaus Cella, Kioto (1992)
Auszeichnung: Preis der Biennale in Venedig 1985
Anschrift: Takamatsu & Lahyani, 36-4 Jyobodaiin-cho, Takeda Fushimi-ku, Kioto, Japan 612. Fax 075-621-6079

Né en 1948 à Shimane. Diplôme à l'université de Kyoto en 1971. Doctorat en 1980. A son propre bureau depuis 1980. Enseigne à l'académie des arts d'Osaka et à l'université technique de Kyoto
Principales réalisations: Maison Koakine, Hyogo (1977); Origin I, Kyoto (1981); Temple Saifukuji, Kani (1982); Clinique dentaire Ark, Kyoto (1983); Magasin Week, Kyoto (1986); Origin III, Kyoto (1986); Kirin Plaza, Osaka (1986); Magasin Ining 23, Kyoto (1987); Maison Syntax, Kyoto (1990); Maison Solaris, Amagasaki (1988); Magasin Oxy, Kyoto (1989); Magasin Imanishi Motoakasaka, Tokyo (1991); Magasin Cella, Kyoto (1992)
Récompense: prix de la Biennale de Venise en 1985
Adresse: Takamatsu & Lahyani, 36-4 Jyobodaiin-cho, Takeda Fushimi-ku, Kyoto, Japan 612. Fax 075-621-6079

RIKEN YAMAMOTO

Born 1945 in Yokohama. Degree from the University of Tokyo 1971. Private practice since 1973
Important buildings: Three Houses, Yokohama (1978); Rotunda Building, Yokohama (1988); Hamlet (residence), Tokyo Shibuya-ku (1988); Hotakubo Residential Complex (1991); Ryokoen-toshi Development, Inter-Junction City, Yokohama (1992)

INDEX

Address: Riken Yamamoto & Field-
shop, A 403 Twin Building Daikanyama, 30-3 Sarugakucho Sibuya,
Tokyo, Japan. Fax 03-464-3413

Geboren 1945 in Yokohama. Diplom
1971 an der Universität Tokio. Eigenes Büro seit 1973
Wichtige Bauten: Drei Häuser , Yokohama (1978); Haus Rotunda, Yokohama (1988); Wohnhaus Hamlet, Tokio Shibuya-ku (1988); Hotakubo-
Wohnanlage (1991); Ryokoen-toshi-
Apartments, Inter-Junction City,
Yokohama (1992)
Anschrift: Riken Yamamoto & Field-
shop, A 403 Twin Building Daikanyama, 30-3 Sarugakucho Sibuya,
Tokio, Japan. Fax 03-464-3413

Né en 1945 à Yokohama. Diplôme
en 1971 à l'université de Tokyo. A
son propre bureau depuis 1973
Réalisations principales: Trois Maisons, Yokohama (1978); Maison Rotunda, Yokohama (1988); Maison
Hamlet, Tokyo Shibuya-ku (1988);
Résidence Hotakubo (1991); Ryokoen-toshi apartments, Inter-Junction
City, Yokohama (1992)
Adresse: Riken Yamamoto & Field-
shop, A 403 Twin Building Daikanyama, 30-3 Sarugakucho Sibuya,
Tokyo, Japan. Fax 03-464-3413

CREDITS

The publisher and editors wish to thank each of the architects and photographers for their friendly assistance. Special thanks go to Yasuo Satomi and Gerhard Feldmeyer, who generously shared their knowledge and contacts in the field.

p. 2	© Kiko Mozuna © Photo: Seihan Sato
p. 6	© Katsuhiro Ishii
p. 9	© Tadao Ando © Photo: Hiroshi Ueda
p. 10	© Kazuo Shinohara © Photo: Shinkenchiku-sha, The Japan Architect Co. Ltd., Tokyo
p. 11	© Hiroshi Hara
p. 12	© Arata Isozaki
p. 13	© Arata Isozaki © Photo: Yasuhiro Ishimoto
p. 14-15	© Shin Takamatsu © Photo: Arwed Voß, Hamburg
p. 16	© Kijo Rokkaku © Photo: Tomio Ohashi, Tokyo
p. 17	© Shin Takamatsu
p. 18	© Toyo Ito © Photo: Tomio Ohashi, Tokyo
p. 19	© Toyo Ito
p. 20	© Itsuko Hasegawa © Photo: S. Yamada
p. 21 above	© Riken Yamamoto © Photo: Arwed Voß, Hamburg
p. 21 below	© Itsuko Hasegawa © Photo: S. Yamada
p. 23	© Atsushi Kitagawara, Tokyo © Photo: Arwed Voß, Hamburg
p. 24	© Kisho Kurokawa © Photo: Tomio Ohashi, Tokyo
p. 26	© Grames-Bilderberg, Hamburg
p. 29	© Grames-Bilderberg, Hamburg
p. 30-31	© Arata Isozaki © Photo: Yasuhiro Ishimoto
p. 32	© Fumihiko Maki © Photo: Tashiharu Kitajima
p. 34	© Itsuko Hasegawa
p. 36-37	© Tadao Ando
p. 38-39	© Shin Takamatsu © Photo: Arwed Voß, Hamburg
p. 40	© Riken Yamamoto
p. 45	© Atsushi Kitagawara © Photo Shigeo Ogawa
p. 46-57	© Tadao Ando (© Photo p. 47, 56, 57: Mitsuko Matsuoka © Photo p. 52-55: Hiroshi Ueda)
p. 58-65	© Hiromi Fujii
p. 66-71	© Hiroshi Hara © Photo: Arwed Voß, Hamburg
p. 72-73	© Hiroshi Hara, Tokyo
p. 74-83	© Itsuko Hasegawa (© Photo p. 76, 77 above, 78-79: S. Yamada)
p. 84-88	© Katsuhiro Ishii
p. 89	© Katsuhiro Ishii © Photo: Shinkenchiku-sha, The Japan Architect Co. Ltd., Tokyo
p. 90-101	© Arata Isozaki (© Photo p. 90: Eiichiro Sakata; Photo p. 91-96, 96-97, 98-99, 100-101: Yasuhiro Ishimoto)
p. 102-109	© Toyo Ito (© Photo p. 103: Arwed Voß, Hamburg; © Photo p. 105-107: Retoria, Tokyo)
p. 110-119	© Kisho Kurokawa (© Photo p. 111, 112 below - 117; © Photo p. 118-119: Tomio Oashi, Tokyo)
p. 120-129	© Fumihiko Maki (© Photo p. 121-126, 129: Toshiharu Kitajima)
p. 130-139	© Kiko Mozuna (© Photo p. 131, 136, 137 above: Arwed Voß, Hamburg; p. 132, 134-135, 138 below: Taisuke Ogawa; © Photo p. 133: Fujisuka Mitsumasa; © Photo p. 138 above, 139: Seihan Sato)
p. 140-147	© Kazuo Shinohara (© Photo p. 141-147: Shinkenchiku-sha, The Japan Architect Co. Ltd, Tokyo)
p. 148-159	© Shin Takamatsu
p. 160-167	© Riken Yamamoto (© Photo p. 160, 161, 163: Arwed Voß, Hamburg; © Photo p. 165: Kenichi Suzuki)